Los Angeles Dodgers 2019

A Baseball Companion

Edited by Patrick Dubuque, Aaron Gleeman and Bret Sayre

Baseball Prospectus

Craig Brown and Dave Pease, Consultant Editors
Rob McQuown and Harry Pavlidis, Statistics Editors

Copyright © 2019 by DIY Baseball, LLC.
All rights reserved

This book or any part thereof may not be reproduced or transmitted in any form or by any means, electronic or mechanical, including photocopying, recording, or by any information storage and retrieval system, without permission in writing from the publisher.

Limit of Liability/Disclaimer of Warranty: While the publisher and the author have used their best efforts in preparing this book, they make no representations or warranties with respect to the accuracy or completeness of the contents of this book and specifically disclaim any implied warranties of merchantability or fitness for a particular purpose. No warranty may be created or extended by sales representatives or written sales materials. The advice and strategies contained herein may not be suitable for your situation. You should consult with a professional where appropriate. Neither the publisher nor the author shall be liable for any loss of profit or any other commercial damages, including but not limited to special, incidental, consequential, or other damages.

Library of Congress Cataloging-in-Publication Data:
paperback
ISBN-13: 978-1-949332-40-7

Project Credits
Cover Design: Kathleen Dyson
Interior Design and Production: Jeff Pease, Dave Pease
Layout: Jeff Pease, Dave Pease

Baseball icon courtesy of Uberux, from https://www.shareicon.net/author/uberux

Ballpark diagram courtesy of Lou Spirito/THIRTY81 Project, https://thirty81project.com/

Manufactured in the United States of America
10 9 8 7 6 5 4 3 2 1

Table of Contents

Foreword v
    Rob Mains

Statistical Introduction vii

Part 1: Team Analysis

Table for Two: Previewing the 2019 Los Angeles Dodgers 3
    Bryan Grosnick and Jason Takefman

Performance Graphs 7

2018 Team Performance 8

2019 Team Projections 9

Team Personnel 10

Dodger Stadium Stats 11

Dodgers Team Analysis 13

Part 2: Player Analysis

Dodgers Player Analysis 18

Dodgers Prospects 87

Part 3: Featured Articles

The Hole in The Shift is Fixing Itself 101
    Russell Carleton

The State of the Quality Start 105
    Rob Mains

Heads-Up Hacking—The First Pitch 111
    Matthew Trueblood

A Hymn for the Index Stat 117
    Patrick Dubuque

Index of Names 121

Foreword

Rob Mains

Welcome to this companion of the 2019 Los Angeles Dodgers. We at Baseball Prospectus are excited to provide this analysis of the Dodgers.

Our website, Baseball Prospectus, is a leader in delivering high-quality commentary and data to baseball fans everywhere. To some, those words—commentary and data—appear mutually exclusive. There are people out there who believe that traditional analysis and advanced analytics must run on different paths. But the simplistic narrative of stats vs. traditionalists just isn't true. Every team's analytics department interacts with scouting, development, and major league operations with a common goal: Delivering a championship. New technologies, like radar tracking of pitch speeds and movement, enable talent evaluators to focus on qualitative aspects of pitching like mechanics and pitch sequencing. In-game strategies like infield shifts, based on batters' hit tendencies, help turn balls in play into outs. Hitters use information to adjust their swings to maximize run production.

All these numbers can seem, at best, intimidating, and at worst, counterproductive to the casual fan. Even as technology and analysis have embedded themselves deeply into the way teams run, it can often feel like statistics create a displacement between the viewer and the sport, breaking them out of the action. And yet every fan incorporates the numbers to some degree; stats like batting average and earned run average, so fundamental to how we talk about performance, are actually complicated formulas. They don't bother people because those formulas have become second nature, as easy to translate as the action on the field.

Along the way, new statistics have entered baseball's lexicon. You'll see some of them, like on-base percentage (which measures a batter's ability to get on base via walk, hit batter, or hit), OPS (on-base plus slugging), and average exit velocity (the speed of balls off a hitter's bat) on broadcasts. Others, like DRC+, might well be new to you. Some of them have been well-defined to the public, others haven't. That lack of context has created ambiguity. Fans know that a ball hit 100 mph is scorched, but does that mean extra bases? (Not if it's hit on the ground or high in the air it doesn't.)

Los Angeles Dodgers 2019

For those who are amenable to them, the new statistics can increase the enjoyment and understanding of the game. They can help fans identify when a pitcher is tiring, when a stolen base or a bunt attempt makes sense (and, more often, when it doesn't), or how a team's lineup might be constructed. Websites like Baseball Prospectus add to that understanding by weaving metrics into the narrative of the game. That's the goal of this publication: to take some of the newer, more complicated statistics and make them as intuitive as the ones on the back of old baseball cards.

But you don't need to love analytics to love baseball. The fans at BP who worked together to write this guide are captivated first and foremost by the game itself. We're drawn to Aaron Judge's power, Francisco Lindor's glove, Billy Hamilton's speed and Patrick Corbin's slider and don't need numbers to tell us why they're so mesmerizing. The underlying statistics provide depth to the game that we all love.

We hope you'll find that this guide helps you better understand the Dodgers. Our analysts have studied the team's major league personnel and its minor league affiliates to identify their strengths and weaknesses, both the obvious ones and those that only a careful dissection of players' performances—yes, including the data—can reveal. You don't need us to tell you who was good and who wasn't in 2018, but our models and writers can help you project how each player is going to perform this year and beyond, and appreciate the greatness of each new game as it unfolds. As in the sport itself, the human and analytic components combine to generate a deeper overall understanding.

Think back to the first time you saw a baseball game on a high-definition TV. You'd grown familiar with how the game looked and felt on a picture tube. But new TV allowed you to see details that you'd never seen before. That's how advanced statistics work. The game itself is why you're here and why you're buying this. (And, for that matter, why we wrote it.) The statistical measures provide the sharper focus, the detail, the depth of knowledge that you didn't have before, generating an overall superior picture. Enjoy the view.

—Rob Mains is an author of Baseball Prospectus.

Statistical Introduction

Sports are, fundamentally, a blend of athletic endeavor and storytelling. Baseball, like any other sport, tells its stories in so many ways: in the arc of a game from the stands or a season from the box scores, in photos, or even in numbers. At Baseball Prospectus, we understand that statistics don't replace observation or any of baseball's stories, but complement everything else that makes the game so much fun.

What stats help us with is with patterns and precision, variance and value. This book can help you learn things you may not see from watching a game or hundred, whether it's the path of a career over time or the breadth of the entire MLB. We'd also never ask you to choose between our numbers and the experience of viewing a game from the cheap seats or the comfort of your home; our publication combines running the numbers with observations and wisdom from some of the brightest minds we can find. But if you *do* want to learn more about the numbers beyond what's on the backs of player jerseys, let us help explain.

Offense

At the end of this past year, we've revised our methodology for determining batting value. Long-time readers of Baseball Prospectus will notice that we've retired True Average in favor of a new metric: Deserved Runs Created Plus (DRC+). Developed by Jonathan Judge and our stats team, this statistic measures everything a player does at the plate–reaching base, hitting for power, making outs, and moving runners over–and puts it on a scale where 100 equals league-average performance. A DRC+ of 150 is terrific, a DRC+ of 100 is average, and a DRC+ of 75 means you better be an excellent defender.

DRC+ also does a better job than any of our previous metrics in taking contextual factors into account. The model adjusts for how the park affects performance, but also for things like the talent of the opposing pitcher, value of different types of batted-ball events, league, temperature, and other factors. It's able to describe a player's expected offensive contribution than any other statistic we've found over the years, and also does a better job of predicting future performance as well.

The other aspect of run-scoring is baserunning, which we quantify using Baserunning Runs. BRR not only records the value of stolen bases (or getting caught in the act), but also accounts for a runner's ability to go first to third on a single or advance on a fly ball.

Defense

Where offensive value is *relatively* easy to identify and understand, defensive value is ... not. Over the past dozen years, the sabermetric community has focused mostly on stats based on zone data: a real-live human person records the type of batted ball and estimated landing location, and models are created that give expected outs. From there, you can compare fielders' actual outs to those expected ones. Simple, right?

Unfortunately, zone data has two major issues. First, zone data is recorded by commercial data providers who keep the raw data private unless you pay for it. (All the statistics we build in this book and on our website use public data as inputs.) That hurts our ability to test assumptions or duplicate results. Second, over the years it has become apparent that there's quite a bit of "noise" in zone-based fielding analysis. Sometimes the conclusions drawn from zone data don't hold up to scrutiny, and sometimes the different data provided by different providers don't look anything alike, giving wildly different results. Sometimes the hard-working professional stringers or scorers might unknowingly inflict unconscious bias into the mix: for example good fielders will often be credited with more expected outs despite the data, and ballparks with high press boxes tend to score more line drives than ones with a lower press box.

Enter our Fielding Runs Above Average (FRAA). For most positions, FRAA is built from play-by-play data, which allows us to avoid the subjectivity found in many other fielding metrics. The idea is this: count how many fielding plays are made by a given player and compare that to expected plays for an average fielder at their position (based on pitcher ground-ball tendencies and batter handedness). Then we adjust for park and base-out situations.

When it comes to catchers, our methodology is a little different thanks to the laundry list of responsibilities they're tasked with beyond just, well, catching and throwing the ball. By now you've probably heard about "framing" or the art of making umpires more likely to call balls outside the strike zone for strikes. To put this into one tidy number, we incorporate pitch tracking data (for the years it exists) and adjust for important factors like pitcher, umpire, batter, and home-field advantage using a mixed-model approach. This grants us a number for how many strikes the catcher is personally adding to (or subtracting from) his pitchers' performance ... which we then convert to runs added or lost using linear weights.

Framing is one of the biggest parts of determining catcher value, but we also take into account blocking balls from going past, whether a scorer deems it a passed ball or a wild pitch. We use a similar approach–one that really benefits from the pitch tracking data that tells us what ends up in the dirt and what doesn't. We also include a catcher's ability to prevent stolen bases and how well they field balls in play, and *finally* we come up with our FRAA for catchers.

Pitching

Both pitching and fielding make up the half of baseball that isn't run scoring: run prevention. Separating pitching from fielding is a tough task, and most recent pitching analysis has branched off from Voros McCracken's famous (and controversial) statement, "There is little if any difference among major-league pitchers in their ability to prevent hits on balls hit in the field of play." The research of the analytic community has validated this to some extent, and there are a host of "defense-independent" pitching measures that have been developed to try and extricate the effect of the defense behind a hurler from the pitcher's work.

Our solution to this quandry is Deserved Run Average (DRA), our core pitching metric. DRA looks like earned run average (ERA), the tried-and-true pitching stat you've seen on every baseball broadcast or box score from the past century, but it's very different. To start, DRA takes an event-by-event look at what the pitchers does, and adjusts the value of that event based on different environmental factors like park, batter, catcher, umpire, base-out situation, run differential, inning, defense, home field advantage, pitcher role, and temperature. That mixed model gives us a pitcher's expected contribution, similar to what we do for our DRC+ model for hitters and FRAA model for catchers. (Oh, and we also consider the pitcher's effect on basestealing and on balls getting past the catcher.)

It's important to note that DRA is set to the scale of runs allowed per nine innings (RA9) instead of ERA, which makes DRA's scale slightly higher than ERA's. The reason for this is because ERA tends to overrate three types of pitchers:

1. Pitchers who play in parks where scorers hand out more errors. Official scorers differ significantly in the frequency at which they assign errors to fielders.
2. Ground-ball pitchers, because a substantial proportion of errors occur on grounders.
3. Pitchers who aren't very good. Better pitchers often allow fewer unearned runs than bad pitchers, because good pitchers tend to find ways to get out of jams.

Since the last time you picked up an edition of this book, we've also made a few minor changes to DRA to make it better. Recent research into "tunneling"–the act of throwing consecutive pitches that appear similar from a batter's point of view until after the swing decision point–data has given us a new contextual factor to account for in DRA: plate distance. This refers to the distance between successive pitches as they approach the plate, and while it has a smaller effect than factors like velocity or whiff rate, it still can help explain pitcher strikeout rate in our model.

New Pitching Metrics for 2019

We're including a few "new" pitching metrics for 2019's suite of Baseball Prospectus publications, but you may be familiar with them if you've spent time scouring the internet for stats.

Fastball Percentage

Our fastball percentage (FB%) statistic measures how frequently a pitcher throws a pitch classified as a "fastball," measured as a percentage of overall pitches thrown. We qualify three types of fastballs:

1. The traditional four-seam fastball;
2. The two-seam fastball or sinker;
3. "Hard cutters," which are pitches that have the movement profile of a cut fastball and are used as the pitcher's primary offering or in place of a more traditional fastball.

For example, a pitcher with a FB% of 67 throws any combination of these three pitches about two-thirds of the time.

Whiff Rate

Everybody loves a swing and a miss, and whiff rate (WHF) measures how frequently pitchers induce a swinging strike. To calculate WHF, we add up all the pitches thrown that ended with a swinging strike, then divide that number by a pitcher's total pitches thrown. Most often, high whiff rates correlate with high strikeout rates (and overall effective pitcher performance).

Called Strike Probability

Called Strike Probability (CSP) is a number that represents the likelihood that all of a pitcher's pitches will be called a strike while controlling for location, pitcher and batter handedness, umpire and count. Here's how it works: on each pitch, our model determines how many times (out of 100) that a similar pitch was called for a strike given those factors mentioned above, and when normalized for each batter's strike zone. Then we average the CSP for all pitches thrown by a pitcher in a season, and that gives us the yearly CSP percentage you see in the stats boxes.

As you might imagine, pitchers with a higher CSP are more likely to work in the zone, where pitchers with a lower CSP are likely locating their pitches outside the normal strike zone, for better or for worse.

Projections

Many of you aren't turning to this book just for a look at what a player has done, but for a look at what a player is going to do: the PECOTA projections. PECOTA, initially developed by Nate Silver (who has moved on to greater fame as a political analyst), consists of three parts:

1. Major-league equivalencies, which use minor-league statistics to project how a player will perform in the major leagues;
2. Baseline forecasts, which use weighted averages and regression to the mean to estimate a player's current true talent level; and
3. Aging curves, which uses the career paths of comparable players to estimate how a player's statistics are likely to change over time.

With all those important things covered, let's take a look at what's in the book this year.

Team Prospectus

You bought this book to learn more about your favorite (or maybe least-favorite, who are we to judge?) team, so let's talk about them. After a thoughtful preview of the 2019 season, you'll be presented with our Team Prospectus. This outlines many of the key statistics for each team's 2018 season, as well as a very inviting stadium diagram.

First you'll find the Performance Graphs page. The first is the 2018 Hit List Ranking. This shows our Hit List Rank for the team on each day of the 2018 season and is intended to give you a picture of the ups and downs of the team's season, including their highest and lowest ranks of the year. Hit List Rank measures overall team performance and drives the Hit List Power Rankings at the baseballprospectus.com website.

The second graph is Committed Payroll and helps you see how the team's payroll has compared to the MLB and divisional average payrolls over time. Payroll figures are currents as of January 1, 2019; with so many free agents still unsigned as of this writing, the final 2018 figure will likely be significantly different for many teams. (In the meantime, you can always find the most current data at Baseball Prospectus' Cot's Baseball Contracts page.)

The third graph is Farm System Ranking and displays how the Baseball Prospectus prospect team has ranked the organization's farm system since 2007. It also indicates the highest and lowest ranks that the farm system achieved over that time.

We start the Team Performance page with the squad's unadjusted and third-order 2018 win-loss records, presented in divisional context. We then list the three highest performing hitters and pitchers by WARP for 2018. Beneath that are a host of other team statistics. **Pythag** presents an adjusted 2018 winning percentage, calculated by taking runs scored per game (**RS/G**) and runs allowed per game (**RA/G**) for the team, and running them through a version of Bill James' Pythagorean formula that was refined and improved by David Smyth and Brandon Heipp. (The formula is called "Pythagenpat," which is equally fun to type and to say.)

Next up is **DRC+**, described earlier, to indicate the overall hitting ability of the team either above or below league-average. Run prevention on the pitching side is covered by **DRA** (also mentioned earlier) and another metric: Fielding Independent Pitching (**FIP**), which calculates another ERA-like statistic based on strikeouts, walks, and home runs recorded. Defensive Efficiency Rating (**DER**) tells us the percentage of balls in play turned into outs for the team, and is a quick fielding shorthand that rounds out run prevention.

After that, we have several measures related to roster composition, as opposed to on-field performance. **B-Age** and **P-Age** tell us the average age of a team's batters and pitchers, respectively. **Salary** is the combined team payroll for all on-field players, and Doug Pappas' Marginal Dollars per Marginal Win (**M$/MW**) tells us how much money a team spent to earn production above replacement level.

Ending this batch of statistics is the number of disabled list days a team had over the season (**DL Days**) and the amount of salary paid to players on the disabled list (**$ on DL**); this final number is expressed as a percentage of total payroll.

Next to each of these stats, we've listed each team's MLB rank in that category from 1st to 30th. In this, 1st always indicates a positive outcome and 30th a negative outcome, except in the case of salary–1st is highest.

The Team Projections page is intended to convey the team's operational capacity entering the 2019 season. We start with the team's PECOTA projected record for 2019, again in divisional context. The **+/-** column indicates how many more or less wins the team is projected to get than they got in 2018. We then list the three highest projected hitters and pitchers by WARP for 2018. A brief farm system summary follows, with the team's top prospect and number of BP Top 101 Prospects. Finally, we list the key new players and departed players, along with their 2019 projected WARP.

Alex Bregman 3B

Born: 03/30/94 Age: 25 Bats: R Throws: R
Height: 6'0" Weight: 180 Origin: Round 1, 2015 Draft (#2 overall)

YEAR	TEAM	LVL	AGE	PA	R	2B	3B	HR	RBI	BB	K	SB	CS	AVG/OBP/SLG
2016	CCH	AA	22	285	54	16	2	14	46	42	26	5	3	.297/.415/.559
2016	FRE	AAA	22	83	17	6	0	6	15	5	12	2	1	.333/.373/.641
2016	HOU	MLB	22	217	31	13	3	8	34	15	52	2	0	.264/.313/.478
2017	HOU	MLB	23	626	88	39	5	19	71	55	97	17	5	.284/.352/.475
2018	HOU	MLB	24	705	105	51	1	31	103	96	85	10	4	.286/.394/.532
2019	HOU	MLB	25	675	96	38	3	23	78	73	107	12	4	.272/.359/.463

Breakout: 6% Improve: 52% Collapse: 5% Attrition: 2% MLB: 100%
Comparables: Anthony Rendon, David Wright, Pablo Sandoval

YEAR	TEAM	LVL	AGE	PA	DRC+	VORP	BABIP	BRR	FRAA	WARP
2016	CCH	AA	22	285	172	38.9	.286	1.6	SS(51): -3.4, 3B(11): 1.4	2.7
2016	FRE	AAA	22	83	161	10.0	.333	-1.2	SS(14): 2.1, LF(3): -0.1	0.8
2016	HOU	MLB	22	217	107	9.6	.317	0.5	3B(40): 0.9, SS(6): -0.1	1.1
2017	HOU	MLB	23	626	114	34.7	.311	-1.5	3B(132): 8.7, SS(30): -2.9	3.9
2018	HOU	MLB	24	705	150	72.6	.289	-1.6	3B(136): 5.4, SS(28): -0.4	7.4
2019	HOU	MLB	25	675	125	37.3	.295	0.0	3B 7, SS 0	4.6

After the projections page, we share a few items about the team's home ballpark. There's the aforementioned diagram of the park's dimensions (including distances to the outfield wall), a few important biographical facts about the stadium, a graphic showing the height of the wall from the left-field pole to the right-field pole, and a table showing three-year park factors for the stadium. The park factors are displayed as indexes where 100 is average, 110 means that the park inflates the statistic in question by 10 percent, and 90 means that the park deflates the statistic in question by 10 percent.

Following the ballpark page, we have a **Personnel** section that lists many of the important decision-makers and upper-level field and operations staff members for the franchise, as well as any former Baseball Prospectus staff members who are currently part of the organization.

Position Players

After all that information and a thoughtful bylined essay covering each team, we present our player comments. Each player is listed with the major-league team who employed him as of early January 2019. If a player changed teams after that point via free agency, trade, or any other method, you'll be able to find them in the book for their previous squad.

First, we cover biographical information (age is as of June 30, 2019) before moving onto the stats themselves. Our statistic columns include standard identifying information like **YEAR**, **TEAM**, **LVL** (level of affiliated play) and **AGE** before getting into the numbers. Next, we provide raw, unstranslated numbers like you might find on the back of your dad's baseball cards: **PA** (plate appearances), **R** (runs), **2B** (doubles), **3B** (triples), **HR** (home runs), **RBI** (runs batted in), **BB** (walks), **K** (strikeouts), **SB** (stolen bases) and **CS** (caught stealing). Then we have unadjusted "slash" statistics: **AVG** (batting average), **OBP** (on-base percentage) and **SLG** (slugging percentage).

Just below the stats box is **PECOTA** data, which is discussed further in a following section. After that, it's on to a pithy and always-informative comment written by a member of the Baseball Prospectus staff, before we cover more stats.

The second text box repeats YEAR, TEAM, LVL, AGE, and PA, then moves on to **DRC+** (Deserved Runs Created Plus), which we described earlier as total offensive expected contribution compared to the league average. Next, one of our oldest active metrics, **VORP** (Value Over Replacement Player), considers offensive production, position and plate appearances. In essence, it is the number of runs contributed beyond what a replacement-level player at the same position would contribute if given the same percentage of team plate appearances. VORP does not consider the quality of a player's defense.

BABIP (batting average on balls in play) tells us how often a ball in play fell for a hit, and can help us identify whether a batter may have been lucky or not ... but note that high BABIPs also tend to follow the great hitters of our time, as well as speedy singles hitters who put the ball on the ground.

The next item is **BRR** (Baserunning Runs), which covers all of a player's baserunning accomplishments which includes (but isn't limited to) swiped bags and failed attempts. Next is **FRAA** (Fielding Runs Above Average), which also includes the number of games previously played at each position noted in parentheses. Multi-position players have only their two most frequent positions listed here, but their total FRAA number reflects all positions played.

Our last column here is **WARP** (Wins Above Replacement Player). WARP estimates the total value of a player, which means for hitters it takes into account hitting runs above average (calculated using the DRC+ model), BRR and FRAA. Then, it makes an adjustment for positions played and gives the player a credit for plate appearances based upon the difference between "replacement level"¬–which is derived from the quality of players added to a team's roster after the start of the season¬–and the league average.

Catchers

Catchers are a special breed, and thus they have earned their own separate box which displays some of the defensive metrics that we've built just for them. As an example, let's check out J.T. Realmuto.

www.baseballprospectus.com

YEAR	TEAM	P. COUNT	FRM RUNS	BLK RUNS	THRW RUNS	TOT RUNS
2016	MIA	18935	-8.5	1.8	2.1	-5.6
2017	MIA	18959	5.3	1.7	1.0	9.1
2018	MIA	16399	-0.4	0.9	0.1	0.4
2019	PHI	18448	-1.4	1.5	0.7	0.8

The **YEAR** and **TEAM** columns match what you'd find in the other stat box. **P. COUNT** indicates the number of pitches thrown while the catcher was behind the plate, including swinging strikes, fouls, and balls in play. **FRM RUNS** is the total run value the catcher provided (or cost) his team by influencing the umpire to call strikes where other catchers did not. **BLK RUNS** expresses the total run value above or below average for the catcher's ability to prevent wild pitches and passed balls. **THRW RUNS** is calculated using a similar model as the previous two statistics, and it measures a catcher's ability to throw out basestealers but also to dissuade them from testing his arm in the first place. It takes into account factors like the pitcher (including his delivery and pickoff move) and baserunner (who could be as fast as Billy Hamilton or as slow as Yonder Alonso). **TOT RUNS** is the sum of all of the previous three statistics.

Pitchers

Let's give our pitchers a turn, using 2018 NL Cy Young winner Jacob deGrom as our example. Take a look at his first stat block: the first line and the **YEAR**, **TEAM**, **LVL** and **AGE** columns are the same as in the position player example earlier.

Here too, we have a series of columns that display raw, unadjusted statistics compiled by the pitcher over the course of a season: **W** (wins), **L** (losses), **SV** (saves), **G** (games pitched), **GS** (games started), **IP** (innings pitched), **H** (hits allowed) and **HR** (home runs allowed). Next we have two statistics that are rates: **BB/9** (walks per nine innings) and **K/9** (strikeouts per nine innings), before returning to the unadjusted **K** (strikeouts).

Next up is **GB%** (ground ball percentage), which is the percentage of all batted balls that were hit in the ground, including both outs and hits. Remember, this is based on observational data and subject to human error, so please approach this with a healthy dose of skepticism.

BABIP (batting average on balls in play) is calculated using the same methodology as it is for position players, but it often tells us more about a pitcher than it does a hitter. With pitchers, a high BABIP is often due to poor defense or bad luck, and can often be an indicator of potential rebound, and a low BABIP may be cause to expect performance regression. (A typical league-average BABIP is close to .290-.300.)

After a witty 150ish words on the player like only Baseball Prospectus's staff can provide, it's on to that second stat block, which repeats the YEAR, TEAM, LVL, and AGE columns. The metrics **WHIP** (walks plus hits per inning pitched) and **ERA**

Los Angeles Dodgers 2019

(earned run average) are old standbys: WHIP measures walks and hits allowed on a per-inning basis, while ERA measures earned runs on a nine-inning basis. Neither of these stats are translated or adjusted.

DRA (Deserved Run Average) was described at length earlier, and measures how many runs the pitcher "deserved" to allow per nine innings. Please note that since we lack all the data points that would make for a "real" DRA for minor-league events, the DRA displayed for minor league partial-seasons is based off of different data. (That data is a modified version of our cFIP metric, which you can find more information about on our website.)

Jacob deGrom   RHP
Born: 06/19/88   Age: 31   Bats: L   Throws: R
Height: 6'4"   Weight: 180   Origin: Round 9, 2010 Draft (#272 overall)

YEAR	TEAM	LVL	AGE	W	L	SV	G	GS	IP	H	HR	BB/9	K/9	K	GB%	BABIP
2016	NYN	MLB	28	7	8	0	24	24	148	142	15	2.2	8.7	143	47%	.312
2017	NYN	MLB	29	15	10	0	31	31	201[1]	180	28	2.6	10.7	239	48%	.305
2018	NYN	MLB	30	10	9	0	32	32	217	152	10	1.9	11.2	269	48%	.281
2019	NYN	MLB	31	13	9	0	31	31	186	145	18	2.3	10.7	221	46%	.286

Breakout: 8%   Improve: 29%   Collapse: 28%   Attrition: 6%   MLB: 85%
Comparables: Erik Bedard, A.J. Burnett, CC Sabathia

YEAR	TEAM	LVL	AGE	WHIP	ERA	DRA	WARP	MPH	FB%	WHF	CSP
2016	NYN	MLB	28	1.20	3.04	3.30	3.5	96.3	59.6	12.1	47.2
2017	NYN	MLB	29	1.19	3.53	3.02	5.7	97.2	55.5	14.5	49.5
2018	NYN	MLB	30	0.91	1.70	2.09	8.0	98.2	52.1	16.3	48.4
2019	NYN	MLB	31	1.02	2.91	3.23	3.9	96.6	54.5	14.8	48.2

Just like with hitters, **WARP** (Wins Above Replacement Player) is a total value metric that puts pitchers of all stripes on the same scale as position players. We use DRA as the primary input for our calculation of WARP. You might notice that relief pitchers (due to their limited innings) may have a lower WARP than you were expecting or than you might see in other WARP-like metrics. WARP does not take leverage into account, just the actions a pitcher performs and the expected value of those actions ... which ends up judging high-leverage relief pitchers differently than you might imagine given their prestige and market value.

MPH gives you the pitcher's 95th percentile velocity for the noted season, in order to give you an idea of what the *peak* fastball velocity a pitcher possesses. Since this comes from our pitch tracking data, it is not publicly available for minor-league pitchers.

Finally, we display the three new pitching metrics we described earlier. **FB%** (fastball percentage) gives you the percentage of fastballs thrown out of all pitches. **WhiffRt** (whiff rate) tells you the percentage of swinging strikes induced out of all pitches. **CS Prob** (called strike probability) expresses the likelihood of all pitches thrown to result in a called strike, after controlling for factors like handedness, umpire, pitch type, count, and location.

PECOTA

All players have PECOTA projections for 2019, as well as a set of other numbers that describe the performance of comparable players according to PECOTA. All projections for 2019 are for the player at the date we went to press in early January and are projected into the league and park context as indicated by the team abbreviation. All PECOTA projected statistics represent a player's projected major-league performance.

The numbers beneath the player's stats–Breakout, Improve, Collapse, Attrition–are part and parcel of the PECOTA projections. They estimate the likelihood of changes in performance relative to the player's previously-established level of production, based on the performance of comparable players:

Breakout Rate is the percent change that a player's production will improve by at least 20 percent relative to the weighted average of his performance over his most recent seasons.

Improve Rate is the percent chance that a player's production will improve at all relative to his baseline performance. A player who is expected to perform just the same as he has in the recent past will have an Improve Rate of 50 percent.

Collapse Rate is the percent chance that a position player's production will decline by at least 25 percent relative to his baseline performance.

Attrition Rate operates on playing time rather than performance. Specifically, it measures the likelihood that a player's playing time will decrease by at least 50 percent relative to his established level.

Breakout Rate and Collapse Rate can sometimes be counterintuitive for players who have already experienced a radical change in performance level. It's also worth noting that the projected decline in a player's rate performances might not be indicative of an expected decline in underlying ability or skill, but could just be an anticipated correction following a breakout season.

MLB% is the percentage of similar players who played in the major leagues in their relevant season.

The final pieces of information are the player's three highest-scoring comparable players as determined by PECOTA. All comparables represent a snapshot of how the listed player was performing at the same age as the current player, so if a 23-year-old pitcher is compared to Bartolo Colon, he's actually being compared to a 23-year-old Colon, not the version that pitched for the Rangers in 2018, nor to Colon's career as a whole.

A few points about pitcher projections. First, we aren't yet projecting peak velocity, so that column will be blank in the PECOTA lines. Second, projecting DRA is trickier than evaluating past performance, because it is unclear how deserving each pitcher will be of his anticipated outcomes. However, we know that another DRA-related statistic–contextual FIP or cFIP–estimates future run scoring very well. So for PECOTA, the projected DRA figures you see are based on the past cFIPs generated by the pitcher and comparable players over time, along with the other factors described above.

Lineouts

In each chapter's Lineouts section, you'll find abbreviated text comments, as well as most of same information you'd find in our full player comments. We limit the stats boxes in this section to only including the 2018 information for each player.

Exclusive Player Visualizations

In our constant battle to provide you with new and interesting baseball content you can't find anywhere else, we've added a trio of data visualizations to each hitter's entry in these books and a pair of visualizations for each pitcher.

For hitters, you'll find three new infographics. The first is each player's **Batted Ball Distribution**, which displays the five major sections of the field: LF (left), LCF (left center), CF (center), RCF (right center), and RF (right). The percentage indicated tells us what percentage of batted balls from that hitter fell within that part of the field during the 2018 season. We've also included the hitter's slugging percentage on balls in play (also called **SLGCON**) for that part of the field.

You'll also see two heatmaps: **Strike Zone vs LHP** and **Strike Zone vs RHP**. These heat maps represent a view of the strike zone from behind the catcher. Areas where there is a darker coloration represent the places where a higher percentage of pitches resulted in hits. In other words, the heatmap represents a hitter's "sweet spots" for getting hits against either left-handed or right-handed pitchers, depending on the image.

Pitchers get two images that help explain what their pitches look like from a hitter's perspective: **Pitch Shape vs LHH** and **Pitch Shape vs RHH**. These images show you the shape and the "tunneling" effect of each pitcher's offerings from the batter's perspective. For each type of pitch that a pitcher throws (represented by an indicator shape), there's a set of dots indicating the flight path, where each dot represents a 0.01-second interval. This maps the average trajectory and speed of an offering, ending where the ball crosses the plate. The solid black box represents the regular strike zone, while the gray contour lines indicate the range of locations that a pitcher typically works in.

Below the image, we provide a bit more detailed information about each pitcher's average offering in the **Pitch Types** box. Here, we also list each of the pitcher's major offerings under the **Type** column.

- **Fastballs** (which usually refers to the four-seam variation)
- **Sinkers** and/or two-seam fastballs
- **Cutters** (which could include "hard" cutters like cut fastballs and "soft" cutters that resemble hard sliders)
- **Changeups** (not including most splitters)
- **Splitters** (split-fingered pitches, forkballs, and some split-changes)
- **Sliders** and/or slurves
- **Curveballs** (including spike-curveballs and knuckle-curveballs, as well as some slurvy curves)
- **Slow curveballs** and/or eephus pitches
- **Knuckleballs**
- **Screwballs**

The **Freq** column indicates the percentage of overall pitches that fall into each of those type categories; if a pitcher has a 16.55% score for changeups, then that's the percent of all pitches that he throws as changeups. **Velo** is exactly what you think it is: the average miles per hour for each pitch type. **H Mov** is the number of inches of horizontal movement on the average pitch of that type, while **V Mov** is the number of inches of vertical movement on the average pitch of that type. (At Baseball Prospectus, we measure this over the long flight of the ball and include gravity into the V Mov number in order to give you the most realistic representation of what the pitch *actually* does.)

If you're wondering about the second number in brackets, that's the index for that velocity or movement compared to the league average. Like DRC+, a score of 100 means that the speed or movement is about the same as league average, while a higher score means that there's higher velocity or movement than the league average. Numbers below 100 indicate less velocity or movement than the league average.

Part 1: Team Analysis

Table for Two: Previewing the 2019 Los Angeles Dodgers

Bryan Grosnick and Jason Takefman

JASON TAKEFMAN: So Bryan, interesting task we have previewing a team with six (!) straight division titles, two straight NL pennants, but has lost consecutive World Series, and at home no less! Takes a special type of manager to be able to rally the troops for this season, as well as, ummm, a special type of manager, I suppose, to lead a team to consecutive 5-1 losses in their last game of the season.

At least the Braves had the decency to lose the majority of their World Series on the road….

BRYAN GROSNICK: I'm not one to bag on the Dodgers for their postseason woes; playing the Astros and the Red Sox at the peak of their powers is a tough task for anyone, and the team has done an excellent job of building a competitive roster year after year. But it *kind of* seems like the Dodgers are in a bit of a transitional period, which is pretty weird for a team with a young core of talent and a history of near-term success. So let me pose this question to you: what's the identity of this Dodgers team going into 2019?

JASON: I could tell you what their identity *isn't*, and that's a powerful right-fielder licking, flipping, and breaking bats. Sigh…. Seriously, I think their identity is something between if *Moneyball* had a huge budget, mixing in young studs while continuing to slash payroll as the last of the big contracts (Hill, Ryu, $47M in dead money) expire after the season, and waiting patiently to play a few important games before October starts. In short, they're not going to change a thing and will continue to win! They should have this division locked up early, especially if Colorado falters and moves key pieces, with the other teams in the division struggling to find an identity.

BRYAN: I agree in a sense that the Dodgers picked a "good" year to pull back and trim the payroll and still be in pole position to win their division. Aesthetically and morally, it feels a little gross—shedding Puig and Grandal while refusing to reload with top-tier talent makes me feel that the Dodgers are growing into the role of the "new" Rays. They seem more than willing to use any tool at their disposal to build an analytics-driven team that emphasizes surplus value over putting the best possible product on the field. The real goal is to serve the twin masters of sustainable quality and return on investment. It's just not all that much fun to root for.

JASON: The Dodgers have led all of MLB in per game attendance every year since 2013. That's not a typo. I know what they have been doing is working—hence the 2 World Series—but shouldn't they be trying to sign Bryce and Manny to short term, high AAV deals, to, you know, get that elusive ring?! It's one thing to not want to pay Matt Kemp and Carl Crawford big money, but shouldn't they be trying to put themselves over the top here?

I mean, where's the urgency and romance, a la Theo at the Schillings for Thanksgiving in 2003! Let me ask you: If Arizona called and said 'we will take your $40M of dead and deferred salary this year, you give us Verdugo, Beatty and Hill, we will give you Greinke? Would you do that, and sign Bryce to 3/100?....

BRYAN: Of course I would. I'd do either part of it. I'd sign Manny or Bryce or Keuchel or a combination and trade for Greinke. *I'd try to make this team better for 2019!* I'd sign any of those dudes to a long-term deal. But the team has different priorities, and we have to face it. So let's focus on the positives for a bit. The Dodgers still have one of the most dominant pitchers in baseball, a sure-fire first-ballot Hall-of-Famer anchoring their rotation. So let's talk about their ace… let's talk about Walker Buehler.

JASON: Yes, please. Seldom does a prospect come along that combines a slight frame, power arm, WHIP to die for, 3.5 WARP in his first full-ish season, and a fabulous 74% contact rate on his go-to pitch, his four-seam fastball. Oh, and like you said, a first ballot Hall-of-Famer to talk to between every inning. If I were the Dodgers, I would pull a Crosby-Lemieux and make Walker live with Clayton, but that's just me.

Would you bet $5 Walker throws more than 210 IP this year, including postseason? For context, he threw 176 IP last year at all levels and seasons. One of the cons of having a young arm with a great team is that teams abort their pre-set plans to win NOW, which could have long term damage: see Francis, Jeff; Wood, Kerry; and Prior's Calves, Mark.

I bring up the Greinke trade due to familiarity, friendly term of three years left, ~~and Kershaw has already started showing signs of decline in his advanced and traditional stats, including durability,~~ and Buehler is currently forced into being the number 2, which is a big load to handle. Please do not reply with Ryu or Hill being the #2–they are side dishes with expiring contracts.

Off the mound, do you think Max Muncy is the new Justin Turner, an incredibly late bloomer, but bloom he will, or is his 2018 4.0 WAR and 161 OPS+ a one year wonder? I wonder if they are planning to depend on that production again…

BRYAN: I think that the Dodgers are planning on some production, but not the excellent overall numbers that made Muncy a top-tier offensive player in 2018. His 146 DRC+ is expected to regress to 119 according to our PECOTA projections, which is good but not the offensive cornerstone he was last year. The torrid performance from the start of the year petered out a bit in the second half, but I'd peg him as certainly capable of being an above-average first baseman.

JASON: Ugh, even more reason to insulate themselves by spending some of the ungodly revenue they receive from their sketchy local TV contract on a true impact player not named A.J. Pollock and his .733 second-half OPS the last three years. Another thing a Bryce signing would do is solidify Bellinger as an everyday 1B instead of moving him so much between there and CF. What do you think this year holds for Julio Urias? Roberts said he will begin the year in AAA, but it feels like he is 22 going on 40. He has a Jurickson Profar broken prospect feel to him. Do you think he needs a change of scenery?

BRYAN: Maybe, but there's still a lot of meat on that bone. Urias possessed preternatural pitchability at a young age, and he's projected for almost three strikeouts per walk by PECOTA. The tough part is, of course, making sure he can stay healthy for something near a full season… no mean feat. I don't think that they need to move on from him in order to see him blossom, I just think he needs to get 80+ innings in the majors.

So tell me what you think we remember about 2019 when we get five years down the line? What will be the signature of this upcoming season for the Dodgers?

JASON: I am not a body shamer, but, meat on the bone is very apt to describe Urias. When we're hanging out in 2024, we'll remember 2019 as the year fan apathy seeped in and Dodgers fans got sick of being in the winning friend-zone: Good enough to go far, but not 'courageous' enough to go far enough and make it happen. I distinctly remember when I saw it with the Braves: Game 3 of the 2001 NLCS vs. the D-Backs. The place was empty, and they announced 83% capacity. Yes, it was during their 10th straight postseason, but that visible moment told me that fans were done.

The 2019 Dodgers are eerily similar: That weird TV contract, seventh straight year in the playoffs, Lebron and the Lakers' Free Agency splashes, and lack of urgency from the front office, and I think this will be *their* Game 3 and the end of their aforementioned average attendance zenith.

Which player do you see regressing and being their biggest disappointment? They are so deep I don't know if ONE player who could derail their season, but I am interested to hear your take.

BRYAN: I guess that if we talk about performance regression, it might be Austin Barnes. I've always liked the versatile backstop, but I'm not sure his signature framing ability will continue to carry his value to the levels PECOTA projects. Our signature system posits that he'll not only hit like a league-average hitter, but that he'll continue to be a best-in-class framer. I think it's more likely than not that he underperforms in both areas, in part due to the improving average level of framing across the league.

Is there a guy that you think might disappoint?

JASON: Barnes is a good one, and his leash will be short with the return of Russell Martin. I'm going to say Justin Turner. Yes, he isn't a typical 34 year-old in terms of wear and tear, and his 4.6 average WARP over the last five full seasons is fabulous, but here's what's leading my hunch. 2018's 11.1 FRAA looks like the exception to a slowly descending defensive trendline, and you know what they say about single-year defensive numbers. Second: PECOTA is rosier than the other projection systems, on the bat, signaling that it might be the outlier. And lastly: He is going to miss his bestie #Puigyourfriend.

Not that it'll be a big deal. See you in October!

Performance Graphs

2018 Hit List Ranking

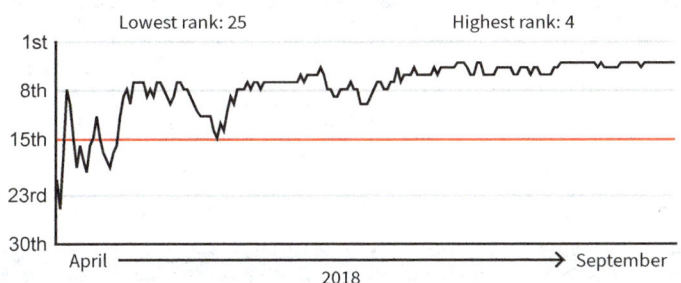

Committed Payroll (in millions)

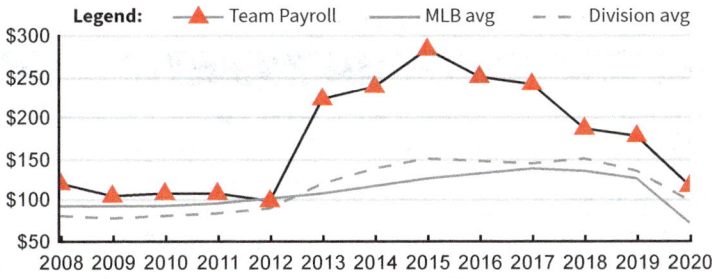

Farm System Ranking

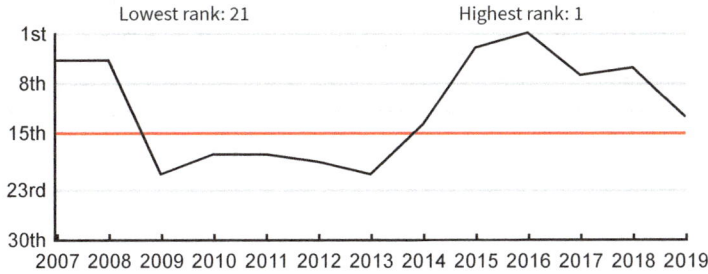

2018 Team Performance

ACTUAL STANDINGS

Team	W	L	Pct
LAN	92	71	.564
COL	91	72	.558
ARI	82	80	.506
SFN	73	89	.450
SDN	66	96	.407

THIRD-ORDER STANDINGS

Team	W	L	Pct
LAN	105	58	.644
COL	88	75	.539
ARI	87	75	.537
SFN	71	91	.438
SDN	66	96	.407

TOP HITTERS

Player	WARP
Justin Turner	5.1
Yasmani Grandal	4.7
Max Muncy	3.9

TOP PITCHERS

Player	WARP
Clayton Kershaw	4.1
Kenta Maeda	3.6
Alex Wood	3.3

VITAL STATISTICS

Statistic Name	Value	Rank
Pythagenpat	.626	3rd
Runs Scored per Game	4.93	5th
Runs Allowed per Game	3.74	2nd
Deserved Runs Created Plus	106	5th
Deserved Run Average	3.48	2nd
Fielding Independent Pitching	3.56	2nd
Defensive Efficiency Rating	.715	6th
Batter Age	28.0	15th
Pitcher Age	29.1	21st
Salary	$186.2M	3rd
Marginal $ per Marginal Win	$4.0M	14th
Disabled List Days	$1,486.0M	27th
$ on DL	17%	16th

2019 Team Projections

PROJECTED STANDINGS

Team	W	L	Pct	+/-
LAN	**93**	**69**	**.574**	**+1**
COL	84	78	.518	-7
ARI	81	81	.500	-1
SDN	79	83	.487	+13
SFN	73	89	.450	0

TOP PROJECTED HITTERS

Player	WARP
Austin Barnes	4.0
Justin Turner	3.8
Cody Bellinger	3.4

TOP PROJECTED PITCHERS

Player	WARP
Clayton Kershaw	2.9
Ross Stripling	2.2
Walker Buehler	2.1

FARM SYSTEM REPORT

Top Prospect	Number of Top 101 Prospects
Alex Verdugo, #19	4

KEY DEDUCTIONS

Player	WARP
Yasmani Grandal	4.2
Manny Machado	3.6
Brian Dozier	2.5
Yasiel Puig	2.4
Alex Wood	1.4
Matt Kemp	0.7

KEY ADDITIONS

Player	WARP
A.J. Pollock	1.9
Russell Martin	0.6
Joe Kelly	0.4

Team Personnel

President, Baseball Operations
Andrew Friedman

General Manager
Farhan Zaidi

SVP, Baseball Operations
Josh Byrnes

Manager
Dave Roberts

BP Alumni
Josh Herzenberg

Dodger Stadium Stats

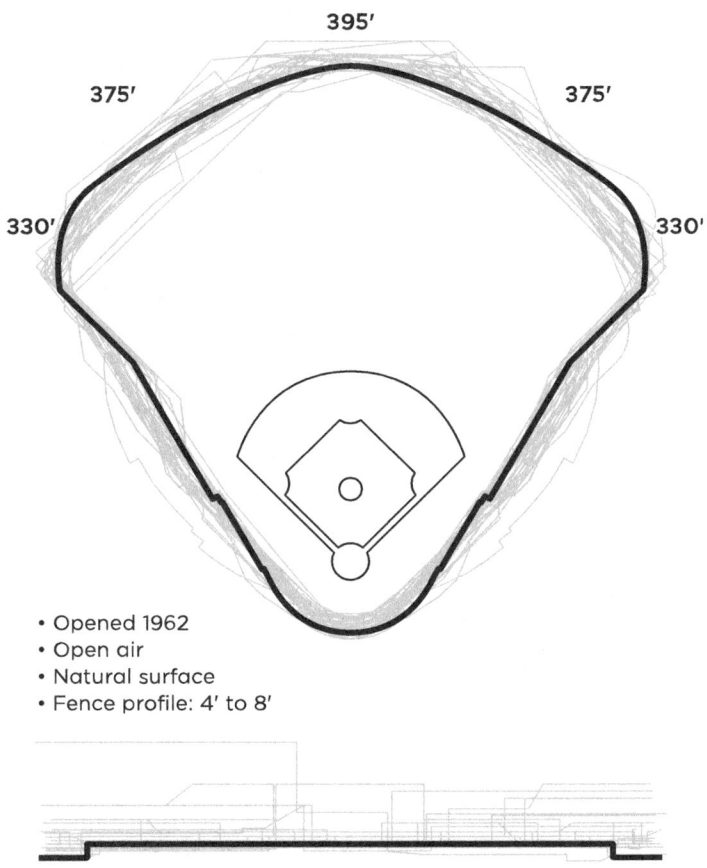

- Opened 1962
- Open air
- Natural surface
- Fence profile: 4' to 8'

Three-Year Park Factors

Runs	Runs/RH	Runs/LH	HR/RH	HR/LH
95	94	99	97	109

Dodgers Team Analysis

The Dodgers are traveling dual paths, as they're both in the middle of one of the most successful runs the team has had since moving to Los Angeles in 1958 and yet still searching for an end to a championship drought that has reached an even 30 years. This offseason presented an extra challenge for the franchise, one of transition, making this arguably the most important offseason under the current ownership group.

Guggenheim Partners took over the Dodgers in May 2012. The team has reached the playoffs in each of the six full seasons since, unprecedented in franchise history, and their 565 regular-season wins during that span are the most in baseball by 20 over the second-place Indians. The ultimate prize hasn't yet been claimed by Los Angeles, with the Dodgers getting tantalizingly close by losing the last two World Series, with the pain at times great enough to undermine the accomplishment of actually reaching the Fall Classic, something they hadn't done since winning it all in 1988.

An attempt at a third straight World Series trip for the Dodgers will be without general manager Farhan Zaidi, who took over as the president of baseball operations for the rival Giants. Zaidi's combination of knowledge, baseball acumen and communication skills are nearly unparalleled in the game. Replacing him could be the Dodgers' biggest challenge.

Since Zaidi and president of baseball operations Andrew Friedman joined the Dodgers in November 2014, the club has continued to both win at the major-league level—four straight NL West titles, three straight NLCS trips, and two World Series—and strengthen the infrastructure, regularly ranking among the top 10 farm systems in baseball during their tenure. Since manager Dave Roberts was hired by this group before the 2016 season, the Dodgers' 23 postseason wins are six more than the team had in the previous 27 seasons combined.

With success comes opportunities, and in many cases that means elsewhere. In addition to Zaidi leaving to run the Giants, third base coach and infield instructor Chris Woodward was hired to manage the Rangers, hitting coach Turner Ward left to take the same position with the Reds, assistant hitting coach Luis Ortiz got the hitting coach job on Woodward's staff in Texas and research and development analyst Ehsan Bokhari left after four years to run the baseball R&D department with the Astros.

Los Angeles Dodgers 2019

All of those jobs were promotions except for Ward, who got to be closer to home with his move to Cincinnati. These departures followed last year, when Alex Anthopoulos left the Dodgers' front office to become the Braves' president of baseball operations, and farm director Gabe Kapler left to manage the Phillies. Those losses suggest the Dodgers have been doing something right, at least. The stated goal has always been to compete every year, and to put in place a system to keep the talent pipeline churning. Now they just have to keep it up, with some new cast members, and likely a tighter budget.

Friedman and Zaidi each came from smaller markets in Tampa Bay and Oakland, respectively, and they certainly enjoyed the trappings of a revenue behemoth in Los Angeles. In the first three seasons of the Friedman-Zaidi front office, the Dodgers averaged $268 million in annual payroll, paying a total of $111.7 million in competitive balance tax from 2015-2017. But it wasn't just money that fueled this Dodgers' run of success. The front office also proved adept at finding value in the margins.

Chris Taylor was plucked out of obscurity in Seattle, becoming a key lineup cog while playing all over the infield and outfield. He was acquired in a trade for former first-round pick Zach Lee, who has pitched only 12 1/3 major-league innings. Max Muncy was the shiny new diamond in the rough last season. After spending all of 2017 in the minors following mediocre major-league results with the A's in 2015-2016, Muncy controlled the strike zone and mashed in his breakout season. The 27-year-old infielder started the year in the minors, but still led the Dodgers in both walks (79) and home runs (35), the latter a total surpassed by only nine players in the 135-year history of the franchise. Not bad from a non-roster invitee to spring training signed to a minor-league deal.

Taylor and Muncy weren't alone. *Eighteen* different players (10 hitters, eight pitchers) amassed at least two WARP for the Dodgers last season, five more than any other team. The average MLB team had just shy of seven such players. The Dodgers' depth was a true strength.

Most 2-WARP players in 2018			
Team	Hitters	Pitchers	Total
Dodgers	10	8	18
Braves	9	4	13
A's	9	3	12
Astros	6	5	11

Friedman and Zaidi showed they could work under constraints, too. Last season's depth came with a payroll of just under the collectively bargained threshold of $197 million, which, given the previous five years of Dodgers payrolls, counted as austerity. This maneuver was only possible thanks to a creative trade between the Dodgers and former front office cohort Anthopoulos with the Braves. Mostly an accounting swap of undesirable contracts, the Dodgers reacquired Matt Kemp for Adrian Gonzalez, Brandon McCarthy, Scott

Kazmir and Charlie Culberson. The cash-neutral deal shaved roughly $24 million off Los Angeles' competitive balance tax payroll for 2018, allowing them to get under the threshold.

Though the primary motivation for the trade was financial, the Dodgers also benefited from a bounce-back campaign from Kemp, who made the All-Star team and posted his highest DRC+ (117) since his first go-around with the Dodgers in 2014. In December, Kemp was part of yet another financially-motivated deal, traded to the Reds along with Yasiel Puig, Alex Wood and Kyle Farmer for Homer Bailey and a pair of prospects. This trimmed some excess and helped streamline the depth chart, but more notably shed roughly $16 million off the competitive balance tax payroll.

Much like with Gonzalez in the prior trade with the Braves, Bailey was immediately released as a condition of this deal. The Dodgers didn't so much trade for Bailey, but rather for the $28 million remaining on his contract to offset the salaries headed to Cincinnati. For the second year in a row, the Dodgers made a massive trade that was less about baseball and more about reallocating payroll. Welcome to Econ 101, with Professor Friedman.

Dodgers ownership chose to stay under the threshold in 2018 to both avoid paying competitive balance tax and to reset their penalty rate should they exceed again in the future. When or if the Dodgers decide to spend lavishly again remains to be seen. Per a November report in the *Los Angeles Times*, a document prepared by the team to lure potential investors in 2017 showed the Dodgers projected their payrolls to fall under the competitive balance tax every year through 2022. Even with the caveat that such a document presented projected profits in the strongest possible light and is in no way binding, it's clear there's at least some limit to the Dodgers' spending, which is a change from the first five years of the Guggenheim Partners ownership group.

Expecting another Muncy or another Taylor to come out of nowhere this season probably isn't wise, but there are many ways to add talent. In particular, the Dodgers have been excellent at incorporating young players into the mix in recent years. Last season, standout right-hander Walker Buehler followed the unanimous Rookie of the Year campaigns of Cody Bellinger (2017) and Corey Seager (2016), and even before that Joc Pederson was an impact starter as a rookie in 2015.

In all four years of this front office, the Dodgers have had at least one All-Star-caliber rookie (all but Buehler received made the actual All-Star team in their respective rookie seasons). Buehler, a 23-year-old rookie with all of 110 career minor-league innings under his belt, was the Dodgers' best pitcher in the second half, which means a lot on a team that's had Clayton Kershaw entrenched atop the rotation for nearly a decade. Buehler's 3.3 WARP was the highest by a 25-and-under Dodgers pitcher other than Kershaw since Chad Billingsley in 2010.

The system has developed and churned out young talent, the lifeblood of a successful team. Having key cogs making deflated pre-free agency salaries, including several near the league minimum, goes a long way in keeping a team's payroll below the competitive balance threshold. Building the infrastructure of the organization put the Dodgers at the forefront of improving the nutrition of their prospects, providing healthy and organic meal options at each minor-league level. Other teams followed suit, realizing that improving the odds of even one extra player contributing in the majors far exceeded the cost of implementing the program.

There are limits, self-imposed and otherwise, on major-league payroll and signing bonuses for amateur players, but there are no such limits on what a team can spend on its front office and development staff. The Dodgers have flexed their financial muscle in that infrastructure, adding to player development and beefing up an analytics department that team president Stan Kasten jokingly referred to as the "room of nerds."

Though the Dodgers didn't replace Zaidi this offseason, they did add an assistant general manager in Jeff Kingston, with more than a decade of experience in player development, analytics and various other front office disciplines in Seattle and San Diego. Kingston and a gaggle of others will try to find that next Seager, Bellinger or Buehler, or maybe even the next Taylor or Muncy. But there's a lot of talent already in the cupboard, with a pantry full enough to perhaps make another World Series run or two. One of these times, they might actually win it.

—Eric Stephen is a writer at SB Nation.

Part 2: Player Analysis

Austin Barnes C

Born: 12/28/89   Age: 29   Bats: R   Throws: R
Height: 5'10"   Weight: 190   Origin: Round 9, 2011 Draft (#283 overall)

YEAR	TEAM	LVL	AGE	PA	R	2B	3B	HR	RBI	BB	K	SB	CS	AVG/OBP/SLG
2016	OKL	AAA	26	385	59	22	5	6	39	43	53	18	3	.295/.380/.443
2016	LAN	MLB	26	37	3	1	0	0	2	5	9	0	0	.156/.270/.188
2017	LAN	MLB	27	262	35	15	2	8	38	39	43	4	1	.289/.408/.486
2018	LAN	MLB	28	238	32	5	0	4	14	31	67	4	3	.205/.329/.290
2019	LAN	MLB	29	412	50	18	2	10	43	47	92	8	3	.248/.344/.394

Breakout: 5%   Improve: 36%   Collapse: 16%   Attrition: 30%   MLB: 88%
Comparables: Carlos Ruiz, Francisco Cervelli, George Kottaras

YEAR	TEAM	P. COUNT	FRM RUNS	BLK RUNS	THRW RUNS	TOT RUNS
2016	LAN	819	0.4	0.0	0.0	0.3
2017	LAN	7057	14.8	1.6	-0.5	15.8
2018	LAN	7013	8.3	1.0	-0.1	9.2
2019	LAN	14112	22.1	2.3	-0.9	23.5

In 1993, "Whoomp! (There It Is)" had its time in the sun. Unfortunately Tag Team wasn't back again with another hit, leaving the song as the only notable entry in the group's catalog. Barnes was great in 2017, pairing his unique-for-a-catcher athleticism with uncanny contact skills at the plate. The combination was enough to unseat Yasmani Grandal as the team's starter for the stretch run, and Barnes got the lion's share of the reps behind the dish in the postseason. His follow-up, however, was not inspiring. Barnes tanked offensively, adding almost 12 percentage points to his strikeout rate thanks to a crippling lack of aggression. Despite a paltry swinging strike rate below six percent, Barnes struck out almost a third of the time by saying "no thank you" to nearly half the strikes he saw. His framing numbers behind the plate remained strong, so Barnes should get plenty of chances, but he'll need to heat up the stick in order to avoid the fate of a one-hit wonder.

YEAR	TEAM	LVL	AGE	PA	DRC+	VORP	BABIP	BRR	FRAA	WARP
2016	OKL	AAA	26	385	129	38.3	.335	3.3	C(63): 16.1, 2B(15): 1.3	4.2
2016	LAN	MLB	26	37	78	-1.0	.217	0.3	C(9): 0.2, 2B(7): -0.2	0.1
2017	LAN	MLB	27	262	122	29.5	.329	0.5	C(55): 15.1, 2B(21): -0.1	3.5
2018	LAN	MLB	28	238	74	5.5	.287	1.1	C(61): 10.0, 2B(19): 0.2	1.5
2019	LAN	MLB	29	412	103	21.7	.302	0.1	C 20	4.0

Austin Barnes, continued

Batted Ball Distribution

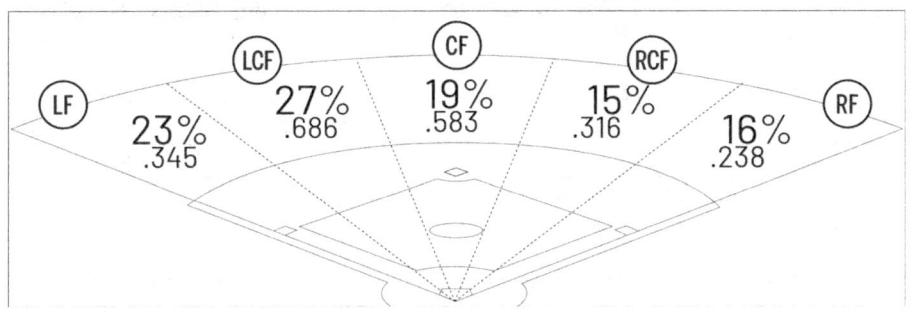

Strike Zone vs LHP

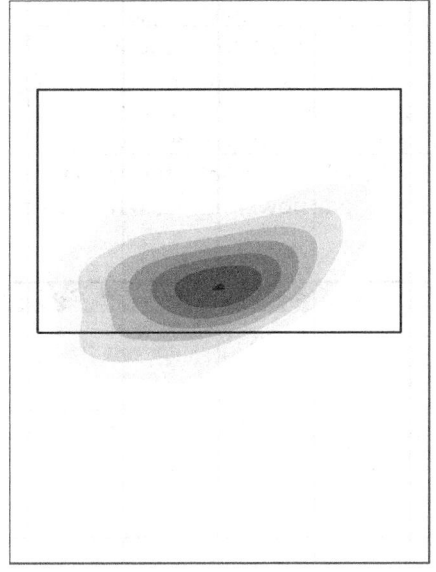

Strike Zone vs RHP

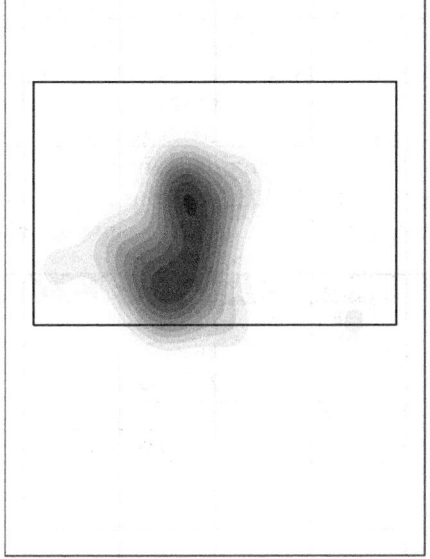

Los Angeles Dodgers 2019

Cody Bellinger 1B
Born: 07/13/95   Age: 23   Bats: L   Throws: L
Height: 6'4"   Weight: 210   Origin: Round 4, 2013 Draft (#124 overall)

YEAR	TEAM	LVL	AGE	PA	R	2B	3B	HR	RBI	BB	K	SB	CS	AVG/OBP/SLG
2016	TUL	AA	20	465	61	17	1	23	65	59	94	8	2	.263/.359/.484
2017	OKL	AAA	21	77	15	4	0	5	15	9	22	7	0	.343/.429/.627
2017	LAN	MLB	21	548	87	26	4	39	97	64	146	10	3	.267/.352/.581
2018	LAN	MLB	22	632	84	28	7	25	76	69	151	14	1	.260/.343/.470
2019	LAN	MLB	23	596	81	26	4	27	84	65	147	12	2	.256/.341/.476

Breakout: 8%   Improve: 58%   Collapse: 12%   Attrition: 6%   MLB: 98%
Comparables: Yasiel Puig, Miguel Cabrera, Freddie Freeman

Beauty is subjective. For some, you're talking about gazing upon the vast majesty of a Grand Canyon sunrise or marveling at the awe-inspiring natural classicism of Michelangelo's *Pieta* in St. Peter's Basilica. For others, it's watching a statuesque slugger uncorking a fluid, looping cut and launching dingers into the stratosphere from the left side. Since his 2017 call-up Bellinger has smashed 64 balls into oblivion, the fourth-highest total in the National League, despite playing around 20 fewer games than his counterparts. While his sophomore campaign didn't produce another top-five National League slugging percentage, Bellinger managed to shave another few percentage points from his strikeout rate, and even started 50 games in center field, contributing above-average defense up the middle. When the dust settles, you've got a versatile, athletic, former NLCS MVP that is one of the most prodigious power hitters in the game. And he's 23 years old. It's a sight to behold.

YEAR	TEAM	LVL	AGE	PA	DRC+	VORP	BABIP	BRR	FRAA	WARP
2016	TUL	AA	20	465	144	32.0	.287	1.0	1B(81): 0.7, CF(13): -0.4	2.1
2017	OKL	AAA	21	77	148	9.0	.450	0.8	1B(16): 1.0, CF(2): -0.5	0.6
2017	LAN	MLB	21	548	129	48.7	.299	-0.2	1B(93): 0.7, LF(39): -2.5	2.9
2018	LAN	MLB	22	632	113	39.0	.313	3.3	1B(110): -0.9, CF(78): 2.0	2.8
2019	LAN	MLB	23	596	121	33.3	.305	1.4	RF 2, 1B -1	3.4

Cody Bellinger, continued

Batted Ball Distribution

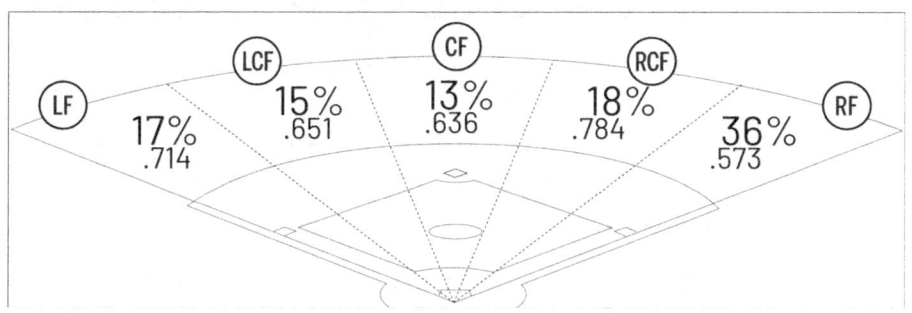

Strike Zone vs LHP

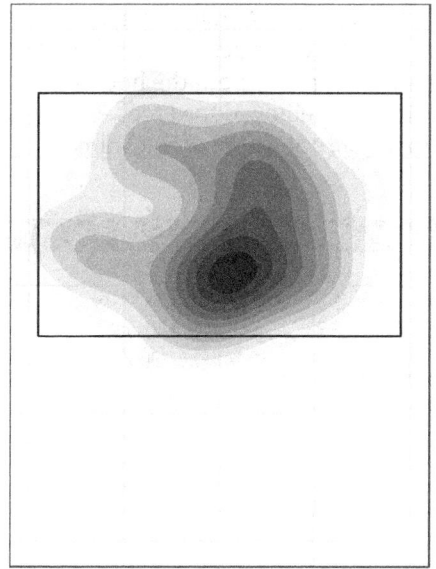

Strike Zone vs RHP

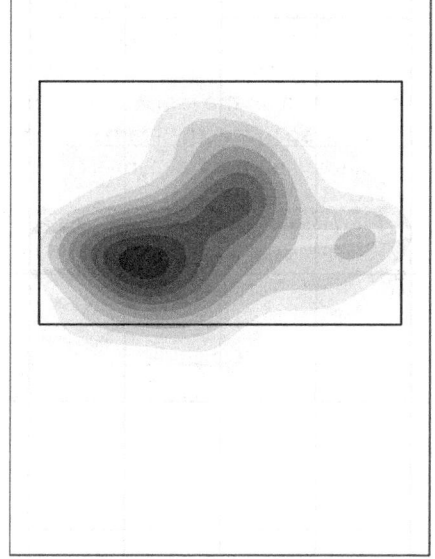

Los Angeles Dodgers 2019

David Freese 3B

Born: 04/28/83   Age: 36   Bats: R   Throws: R
Height: 6'2"   Weight: 220   Origin: Round 9, 2006 Draft (#273 overall)

YEAR	TEAM	LVL	AGE	PA	R	2B	3B	HR	RBI	BB	K	SB	CS	AVG/OBP/SLG
2016	PIT	MLB	33	492	63	23	0	13	55	45	142	0	0	.270/.352/.412
2017	PIT	MLB	34	503	44	16	0	10	52	58	116	0	1	.263/.368/.371
2018	PIT	MLB	35	265	29	10	1	9	42	18	56	0	0	.282/.336/.444
2018	LAN	MLB	35	47	9	2	1	2	9	6	16	0	0	.385/.489/.641
2019	LAN	MLB	36	281	30	11	1	7	31	27	76	0	0	.247/.335/.385

Breakout: 0%   Improve: 14%   Collapse: 18%   Attrition: 22%   MLB: 74%
Comparables: Melvin Mora, Ken Boyer, Casey Blake

In the days of extreme shifts and openers, simple platoon players have somehow fallen by the wayside as far as trendy baseball topics are concerned. It's too bad for the lefty-mashing Freese, who will once again just have to rely on postseason heroics to create buzz for himself. Acquired at the August waiver deadline, Freese proceeded to hit a robust .464 against southpaws for his new club, bringing his career line against lefties to .305/.381/.467. In addition to providing the pop, Freese was an average-or-better defender for the third consecutive season, leaving the days of minus defense at both the hot and cold corners further in the rearview mirror. The Dodgers enjoyed the Freese experience so much, the team inked him to a new, one-year contract almost immediately upon the season's completion.

YEAR	TEAM	LVL	AGE	PA	DRC+	VORP	BABIP	BRR	FRAA	WARP
2016	PIT	MLB	33	492	90	16.6	.372	-0.4	3B(78): 0.2, 1B(58): 3.0	1.0
2017	PIT	MLB	34	503	96	17.5	.336	-4.7	3B(116): 5.3, 1B(3): 0.0	1.6
2018	PIT	MLB	35	265	109	11.4	.330	-0.9	3B(55): 1.7, 1B(15): 1.0	1.3
2018	LAN	MLB	35	47	111	7.0	.619	-0.5	1B(14): -0.4, 3B(3): 0.0	0.0
2019	LAN	MLB	36	281	96	4.6	.324	-0.6	1B 3, 3B 0	0.8

David Freese, continued

Batted Ball Distribution

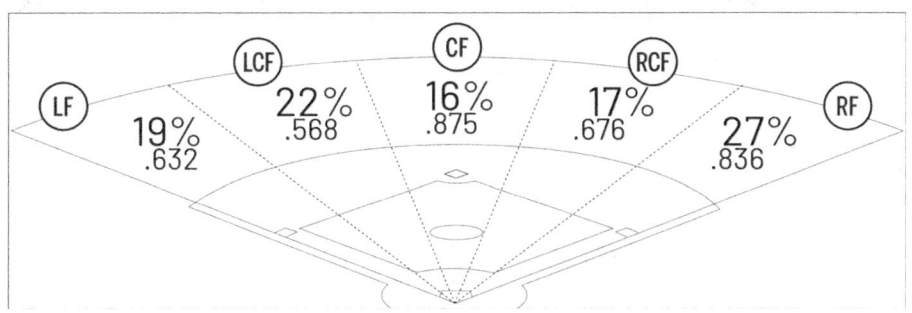

Strike Zone vs LHP   **Strike Zone vs RHP**

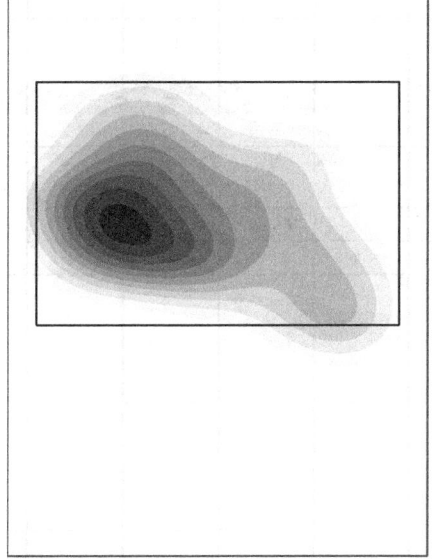

Los Angeles Dodgers 2019

Enrique Hernandez UT
Born: 08/24/91 Age: 27 Bats: R Throws: R
Height: 5'11" Weight: 200 Origin: Round 6, 2009 Draft (#191 overall)

YEAR	TEAM	LVL	AGE	PA	R	2B	3B	HR	RBI	BB	K	SB	CS	AVG/OBP/SLG
2016	LAN	MLB	24	244	25	8	0	7	18	28	64	2	0	.190/.283/.324
2017	LAN	MLB	25	342	46	24	2	11	37	41	80	3	0	.215/.308/.421
2018	LAN	MLB	26	462	67	17	3	21	52	50	78	3	0	.256/.336/.470
2019	LAN	MLB	27	424	51	20	1	14	50	45	88	3	0	.239/.324/.411

Breakout: 11% Improve: 59% Collapse: 16% Attrition: 12% MLB: 100%
Comparables: Nate McLouth, Ryan Sweeney, Chris Coghlan

Enrique, do you love me? Are you riding?
'Cause you're hitting righties now, and I like it
And I need ya, the pop and speed, yeah
You know I'm down for you always
KH, do you love me? I see you're playing
Out there at every single spot on the diamond
'Cause to me you're more than just UT, yeah
And I'm down for you always.

YEAR	TEAM	LVL	AGE	PA	DRC+	VORP	BABIP	BRR	FRAA	WARP
2016	LAN	MLB	24	244	79	0.5	.234	-0.9	LF(41): 2.6, CF(22): -0.7	0.2
2017	LAN	MLB	25	342	89	14.4	.254	2.6	CF(34): 5.8, LF(28): 0.7	1.7
2018	LAN	MLB	26	462	112	29.0	.266	1.9	CF(63): -0.8, 2B(41): -0.3	2.2
2019	LAN	MLB	27	424	100	16.5	.273	-0.2	2B 0, CF 0	1.3

Enrique Hernandez, continued

Batted Ball Distribution

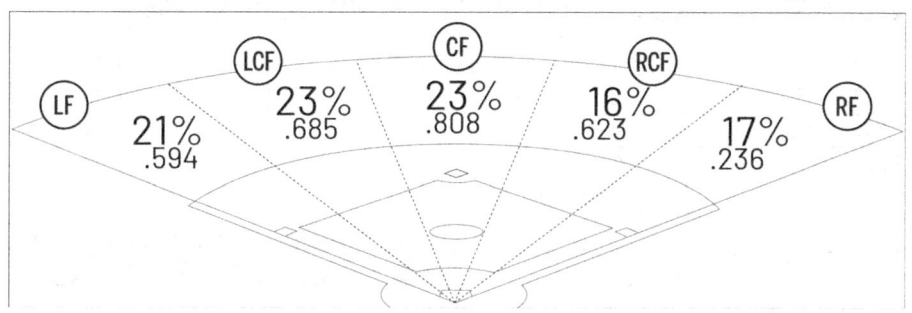

Strike Zone vs LHP

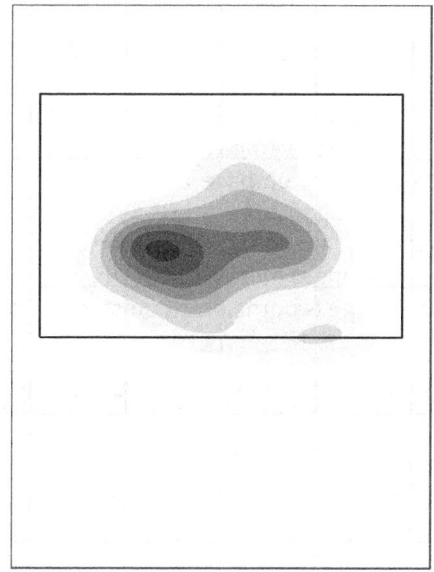

Strike Zone vs RHP

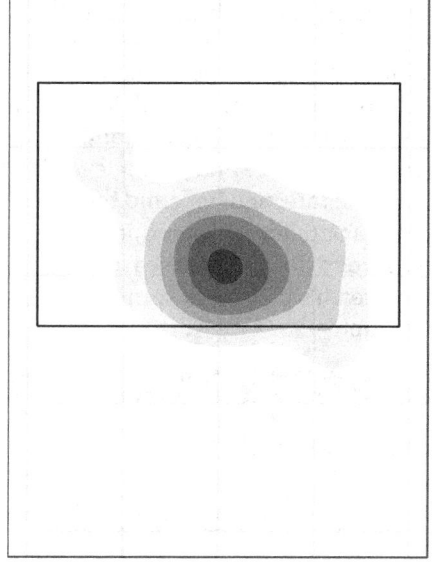

Russell Martin C

Born: 02/15/83   Age: 36   Bats: R   Throws: R
Height: 5'10"   Weight: 205   Origin: Round 17, 2002 Draft (#511 overall)

YEAR	TEAM	LVL	AGE	PA	R	2B	3B	HR	RBI	BB	K	SB	CS	AVG/OBP/SLG
2016	TOR	MLB	33	535	62	16	0	20	74	64	148	2	1	.231/.335/.398
2017	TOR	MLB	34	365	49	12	0	13	35	50	83	1	2	.221/.343/.388
2018	TOR	MLB	35	352	37	8	0	10	25	56	82	0	3	.194/.338/.325
2019	LAN	MLB	36	198	22	7	0	6	22	25	49	1	1	.220/.330/.369

Breakout: 2%   Improve: 24%   Collapse: 23%   Attrition: 20%   MLB: 79%
Comparables: Sherm Lollar, Hank Gowdy, Bill Dickey

You can't go back home to your team, back home to the prime of your career, back home to a young catcher's dreams of glory and fame, to playing just for playing's sake, back home to the old statistics and systems of a game which once seemed everlasting

YEAR	TEAM	P. COUNT	FRM RUNS	BLK RUNS	THRW RUNS	TOT RUNS
2016	TOR	16738	15.8	0.1	-2.8	12.5
2017	TOR	11346	2.6	-0.2	-1.1	1.1
2018	TOR	10485	7.3	1.6	-0.3	8.4
2019	LAN	5932	3.0	0.2	-0.5	2.7

but which is changing all the time. The past is immutable, at least where Tom Wolfe and Father Time are concerned, and never was that fact put into sharper focus than during the fourth leg of Martin's five-year, $82 million deal in Toronto. There's simply nothing outstanding about an above-average receiver with declining average and power, even if he is still getting on-base via the walk at a near-elite rate, and he found himself frequently edged out of starts as Gibbons paved a path for 20-something backstops Danny Jansen and Luke Maile during the second half of a lost season. Martin may no longer match his past, his salary or his team's plans, but sometimes finding a home is borne of circumstance, not geography.

YEAR	TEAM	LVL	AGE	PA	DRC+	VORP	BABIP	BRR	FRAA	WARP
2016	TOR	MLB	33	535	96	19.3	.291	0.3	C(127): 12.9, 2B(1): 0.0	3.6
2017	TOR	MLB	34	365	98	12.8	.261	0.2	C(83): 0.8, 3B(10): 0.7	1.9
2018	TOR	MLB	35	352	94	6.7	.234	-5.1	C(71): 7.6, 3B(21): 0.5	1.7
2019	LAN	MLB	36	198	87	5.4	.274	-0.7	C 2	0.6

Russell Martin, continued

Batted Ball Distribution

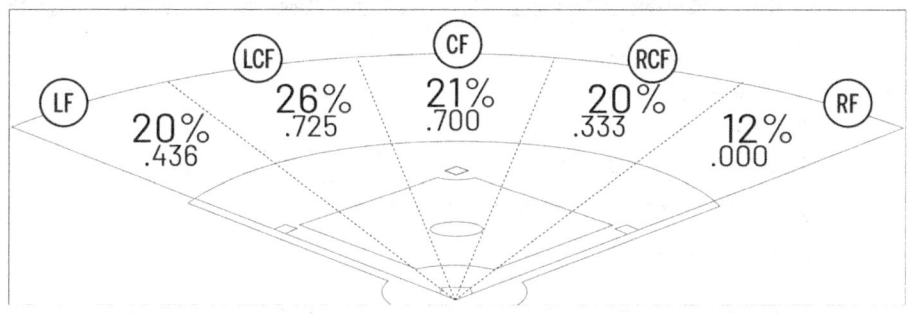

Strike Zone vs LHP

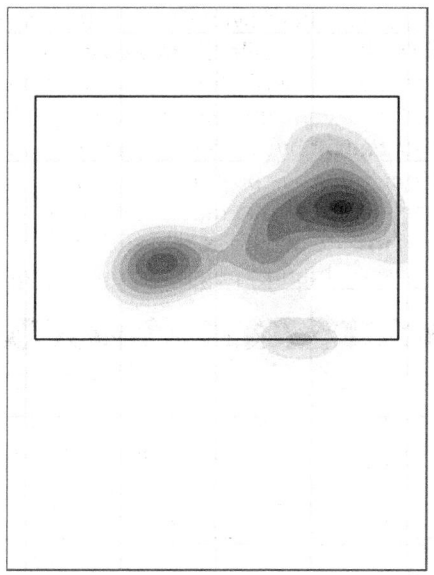

Strike Zone vs RHP

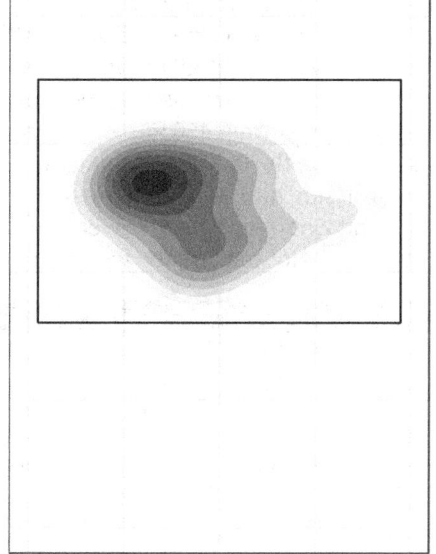

Los Angeles Dodgers 2019

Max Muncy   INF
Born: 08/25/90   Age: 28   Bats: L   Throws: R
Height: 6'0"   Weight: 210   Origin: Round 5, 2012 Draft (#169 overall)

YEAR	TEAM	LVL	AGE	PA	R	2B	3B	HR	RBI	BB	K	SB	CS	AVG/OBP/SLG
2016	NAS	AAA	25	268	34	7	2	8	26	35	54	5	0	.251/.360/.408
2016	OAK	MLB	25	133	13	2	0	2	8	20	24	0	0	.186/.308/.257
2017	OKL	AAA	26	379	62	20	1	12	44	54	84	3	6	.309/.414/.491
2018	OKL	AAA	27	38	7	2	0	2	4	6	5	0	0	.313/.421/.563
2018	LAN	MLB	27	481	75	17	2	35	79	79	131	3	0	.263/.391/.582
2019	LAN	MLB	28	584	85	22	1	27	75	75	148	3	1	.244/.348/.454

Breakout: 4%   Improve: 40%   Collapse: 18%   Attrition: 26%   MLB: 81%
Comparables: Tyler Moore, Chris Shelton, Chris Parmelee

Peter Parker. Bruce Banner. Bucky Barnes. Like his alliterative brethren, Max Muncy swooped to the rescue this season, transforming into an offensive superhero for the injury-riddled Dodgers. Muncy patiently waited seven years for a shot at regular playing time without riding buses, and that patience manifested itself in spades this season with the former Baylor Bear trailing only Mike Trout, Bryce Harper and Joey Votto in walk rate. While the free passes are nice, Muncy also added a shocking amount of thump with the lumber, smacking 24 of his 35 homers in his first 80 games with the team and leading the league in isolated power (min 450 PA). And he topped it all off by bailing the team out with his defensive flexibility, spending time at four defensive positions without embarrassing himself anywhere. With great power comes great responsibility, sure, and when that great power is attached to elite plate discipline, it's easy to get excited. Not too shabby for a mild-mannered, friendly neighborhood castoff.

YEAR	TEAM	LVL	AGE	PA	DRC+	VORP	BABIP	BRR	FRAA	WARP
2016	NAS	AAA	25	268	106	15.1	.291	-0.5	LF(28): -1.3, 3B(13): -1.2	0.0
2016	OAK	MLB	25	133	91	-2.5	.218	0.3	2B(21): 0.3, RF(17): 0.0	0.3
2017	OKL	AAA	26	379	140	36.1	.387	2.0	3B(53): 0.3, 1B(22): 1.9	2.5
2018	OKL	AAA	27	38	132	4.6	.320	0.7	1B(7): 0.1, 3B(3): 0.2	0.3
2018	LAN	MLB	27	481	146	49.5	.299	2.3	1B(84): -0.5, 3B(38): 0.3	3.9
2019	LAN	MLB	28	584	120	29.8	.292	-0.9	1B -4, 2B -2	2.2

Max Muncy, continued

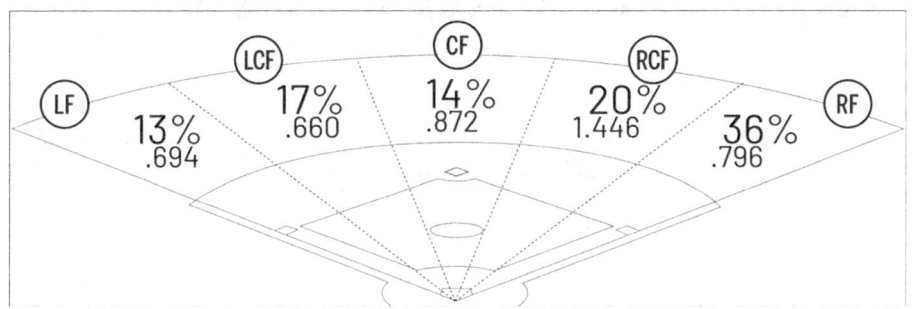

Batted Ball Distribution

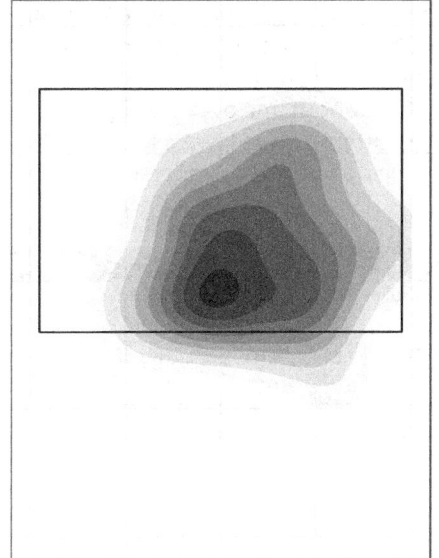

Strike Zone vs LHP

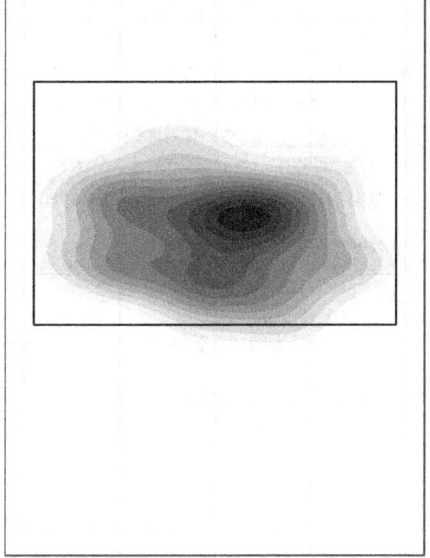

Strike Zone vs RHP

Los Angeles Dodgers 2019

Joc Pederson LF
Born: 04/21/92   Age: 27   Bats: L   Throws: L
Height: 6'1"   Weight: 220   Origin: Round 11, 2010 Draft (#352 overall)

YEAR	TEAM	LVL	AGE	PA	R	2B	3B	HR	RBI	BB	K	SB	CS	AVG/OBP/SLG
2016	LAN	MLB	24	476	64	26	0	25	68	63	130	6	2	.246/.352/.495
2017	OKL	AAA	25	71	8	1	0	3	9	5	14	1	0	.169/.225/.323
2017	LAN	MLB	25	323	44	20	0	11	35	39	68	4	3	.212/.331/.407
2018	LAN	MLB	26	443	65	27	3	25	56	40	85	1	5	.248/.321/.522
2019	LAN	MLB	27	455	62	21	2	18	54	45	100	4	4	.236/.324/.434

Breakout: 8%   Improve: 58%   Collapse: 11%   Attrition: 6%   MLB: 97%
Comparables: Carlos Quentin, Alex Gordon, Nick Swisher

Alexander Pope spoke on expectations: "Blessed is he who expects nothing, for he shall never be disappointed." The expectations were lofty for Pederson, especially after going 30/30 with a .300 batting average at Triple-A in 2014. The lefty followed suit by stealing 15 bases in his four subsequent seasons in the big leagues. No, Pederson would not be going 30/30 anytime soon, and it was probably unfair to expect him to (it's happened only eight times since 2010, and 62 times ever). Despite those inflated expectations, Yung Joc has turned into one of the better righty mashers in the game, putting up a .556 slugging percentage against right-handed pitching. Only about one of every eight Pederson plate appearances came against southpaws, the lowest number of his career, and one that should continue trending downward as Pederson ages. It's all about managing expectations, after all.

YEAR	TEAM	LVL	AGE	PA	DRC+	VORP	BABIP	BRR	FRAA	WARP
2016	LAN	MLB	24	476	115	35.5	.296	-3.6	CF(132): -2.2	1.9
2017	OKL	AAA	25	71	40	-3.9	.163	-0.2	LF(10): 3.7, CF(4): 0.8	0.0
2017	LAN	MLB	25	323	89	14.2	.241	1.8	CF(92): -9.1, LF(4): -0.4	-0.1
2018	LAN	MLB	26	443	118	26.4	.253	0.9	LF(116): -1.3, CF(32): -2.4	1.9
2019	LAN	MLB	27	455	106	17.7	.265	-1.3	LF 0, CF -1	1.6

Joc Pederson, continued

Batted Ball Distribution

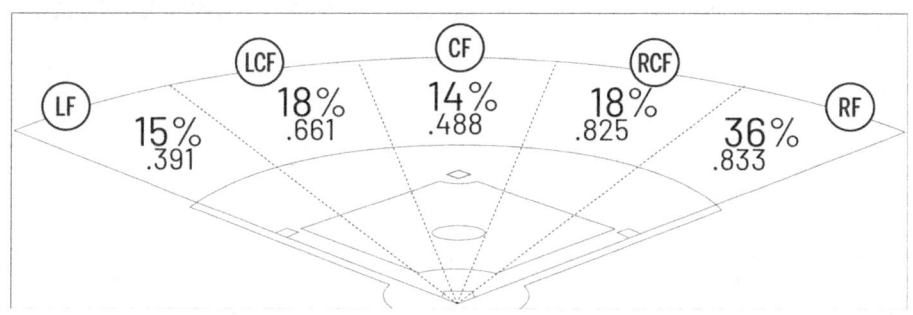

Strike Zone vs LHP   **Strike Zone vs RHP**

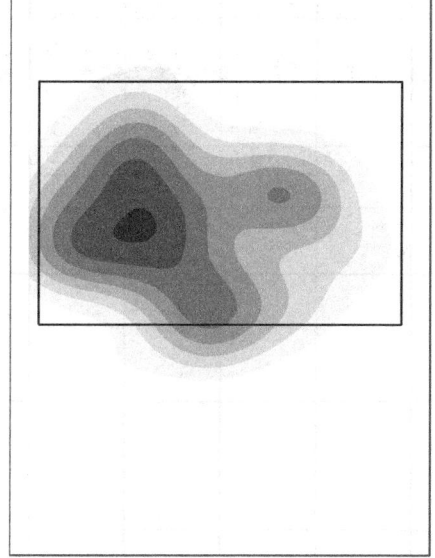

Los Angeles Dodgers 2019

A.J. Pollock CF
Born: 12/05/87   Age: 31   Bats: R   Throws: R
Height: 6'1"   Weight: 195   Origin: Round 1, 2009 Draft (#17 overall)

YEAR	TEAM	LVL	AGE	PA	R	2B	3B	HR	RBI	BB	K	SB	CS	AVG/OBP/SLG
2016	ARI	MLB	28	46	9	0	0	2	4	5	8	4	0	.244/.326/.390
2017	ARI	MLB	29	466	73	33	6	14	49	35	71	20	6	.266/.330/.471
2018	ARI	MLB	30	460	61	21	5	21	65	31	100	13	2	.257/.316/.484
2019	LAN	MLB	31	492	62	25	3	16	58	37	98	19	4	.256/.321/.434

Breakout: 1%   Improve: 41%   Collapse: 10%   Attrition: 4%   MLB: 96%
Comparables: Jacoby Ellsbury, Angel Pagan, Charlie Blackmon

Pollock is set for life either way and was one of this offseason's most coveted free agents, but if he'd just stayed healthy for one more season somewhere along the way he would have gotten *paid*. Instead, he's spent much of the time since his monster 2015 breakout campaign on the disabled list, and when healthy he's more often good rather than great. For now he's among the top 10-12 center fielders in the game, but Pollock seems unlikely to age particularly well and has already shown signs of slipping defensively.

YEAR	TEAM	LVL	AGE	PA	DRC+	VORP	BABIP	BRR	FRAA	WARP
2016	ARI	MLB	28	46	99	2.8	.258	1.8	CF(12): 1.5	0.5
2017	ARI	MLB	29	466	100	28.2	.291	0.7	CF(109): 0.3	1.7
2018	ARI	MLB	30	460	106	23.4	.284	1.1	CF(109): -7.6	1.3
2019	LAN	MLB	31	492	102	22.3	.293	2.4	CF -4	1.9

A.J. Pollock, continued

Batted Ball Distribution

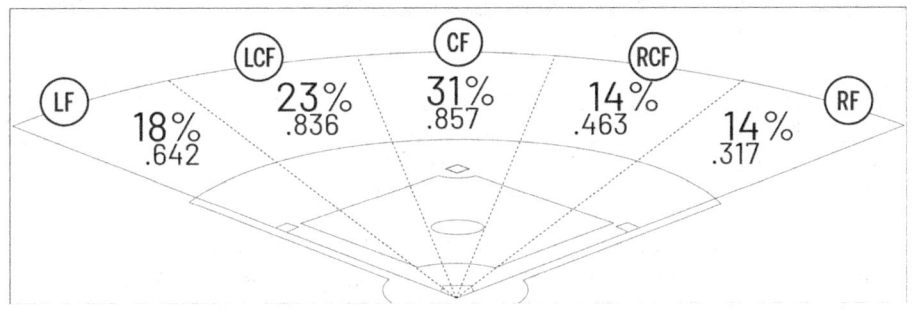

Strike Zone vs LHP **Strike Zone vs RHP**

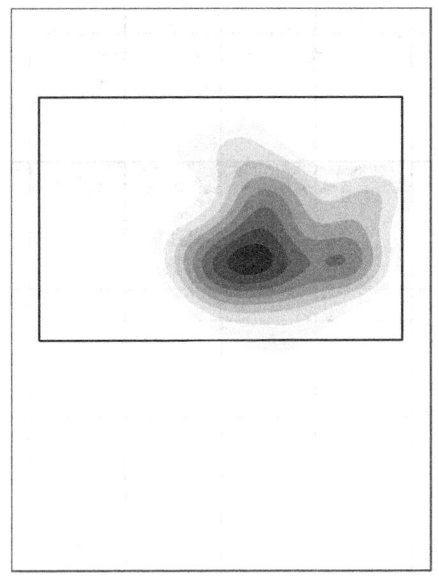 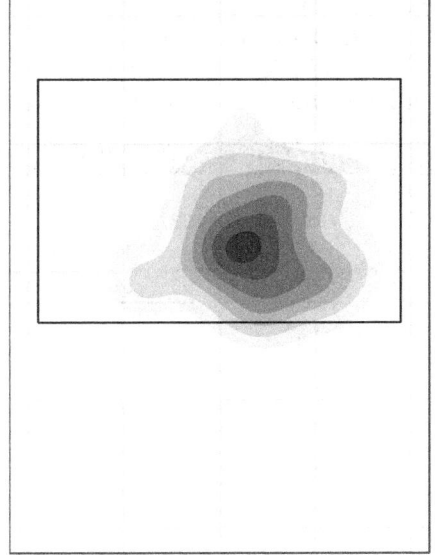

Corey Seager SS

Born: 04/27/94   Age: 25   Bats: L   Throws: R
Height: 6'4"   Weight: 220   Origin: Round 1, 2012 Draft (#18 overall)

YEAR	TEAM	LVL	AGE	PA	R	2B	3B	HR	RBI	BB	K	SB	CS	AVG/OBP/SLG
2016	LAN	MLB	22	687	105	40	5	26	72	54	133	3	3	.308/.365/.512
2017	LAN	MLB	23	613	85	33	0	22	77	67	131	4	2	.295/.375/.479
2018	LAN	MLB	24	115	13	5	1	2	13	11	17	0	0	.267/.348/.396
2019	LAN	MLB	25	571	69	30	2	19	74	51	117	3	1	.281/.350/.459

Breakout: 8%   Improve: 63%   Collapse: 1%   Attrition: 2%   MLB: 100%
Comparables: Troy Tulowitzki, Anthony Rendon, Hanley Ramirez

There's nothing more brutal (from a sports standpoint) than seeing exciting young players lose huge chunks of time due to injury. Seager's 2018 campaign was riddled with more maladies than Cavity Sam from Operation. Lingering hip and elbow pain eventually led to separate surgeries, limiting the shortstop to only 26 games in what amounted to a lost season. While power numbers slowly creeping downward would typically be an alarming trend, we can probably just chalk that up to, you know, playing only 26 games. The injuries could cause whispers of an eventual move off the six to grow into a dull roar, but with a clean bill of health, Seager should once again resume his prodigious hitting, flirting with .300 and 30 homers on an annual basis.

YEAR	TEAM	LVL	AGE	PA	DRC+	VORP	BABIP	BRR	FRAA	WARP
2016	LAN	MLB	22	687	122	73.1	.355	2.7	SS(155): -8.8	4.3
2017	LAN	MLB	23	613	115	58.5	.352	2.2	SS(138): -1.8	4.0
2018	LAN	MLB	24	115	104	7.2	.301	0.8	SS(25): 0.3	0.7
2019	LAN	MLB	25	571	121	40.2	.328	-1.0	SS -6	3.0

Corey Seager, continued

Batted Ball Distribution

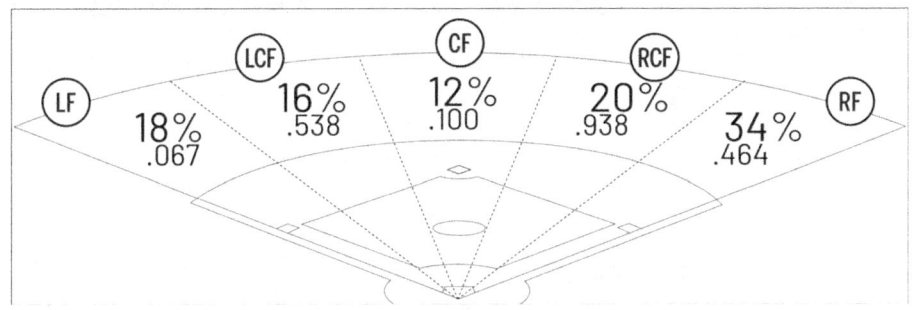

Strike Zone vs LHP   Strike Zone vs RHP

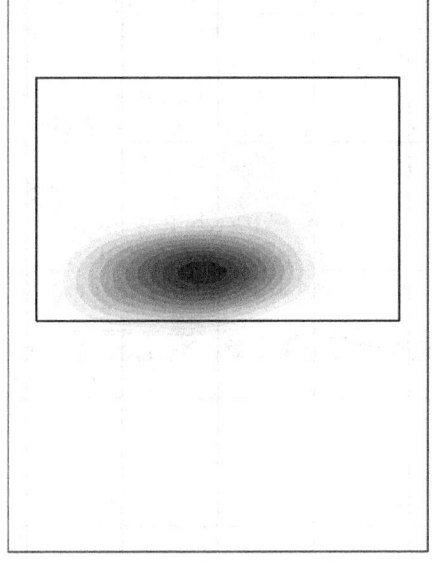

Los Angeles Dodgers 2019

Chris Taylor UT
Born: 08/29/90 Age: 28 Bats: R Throws: R
Height: 6'1" Weight: 195 Origin: Round 5, 2012 Draft (#161 overall)

YEAR	TEAM	LVL	AGE	PA	R	2B	3B	HR	RBI	BB	K	SB	CS	AVG/OBP/SLG
2016	SEA	MLB	25	3	0	0	0	0	0	0	2	0	0	.333/.333/.333
2016	TAC	AAA	25	280	41	19	4	3	29	29	49	12	5	.312/.387/.457
2016	OKL	AAA	25	64	7	6	2	0	8	6	16	5	0	.368/.438/.544
2016	LAN	MLB	25	62	8	2	2	1	7	4	13	0	0	.207/.258/.362
2017	OKL	AAA	26	49	8	2	2	1	5	5	5	1	2	.233/.327/.442
2017	LAN	MLB	26	568	85	34	5	21	72	50	142	17	4	.288/.354/.496
2018	LAN	MLB	27	604	85	35	8	17	63	55	178	9	6	.254/.331/.444
2019	LAN	MLB	28	546	74	28	5	16	58	49	142	12	5	.260/.332/.436

Breakout: 6%   Improve: 46%   Collapse: 14%   Attrition: 20%   MLB: 92%
Comparables: Sean Rodriguez, Brendan Harris, Tim Beckham

After the baseball gods doused him with Dodger development dust upon his arrival, Taylor took a slight step back in his second year with the club. He ran a little, but not quite as much. He smacked a few dingers, but not quite at the torrid clip he set forth in his 2017 team debut. He led the National League in strikeouts (ok, maybe that last one isn't as spinnable). Even if Taylor's 2018 was regression to the mean, the end product was still extremely good. Year Two of the Taylor swing change experiment yielded even more line drives, at the expense of ground balls, and the offensive production paired with above-average defense from four spots on the diamond. Sure, the strikeouts aren't ideal, but the extra whiffs were often the product of working deep into counts, as only 13 National League hitters saw more pitches per plate appearances than Taylor. When a "down-ish" year looks like this, you're pretty close to a star.

YEAR	TEAM	LVL	AGE	PA	DRC+	VORP	BABIP	BRR	FRAA	WARP
2016	SEA	MLB	25	3	74	0.0	1.000	0.0	SS(1): -0.3	0.0
2016	TAC	AAA	25	280	135	20.7	.378	0.0	SS(50): 2.1, 2B(7): -1.3	1.8
2016	OKL	AAA	25	64	137	9.2	.512	1.0	SS(13): -1.2, 3B(2): -0.1	0.4
2016	LAN	MLB	25	62	79	-0.7	.250	0.7	3B(10): -0.1, 2B(7): -0.5	0.0
2017	OKL	AAA	26	49	90	2.9	.243	0.6	SS(5): 0.5, CF(3): 0.2	0.2
2017	LAN	MLB	26	568	114	50.4	.361	4.4	CF(49): -2.2, LF(48): 6.6	3.9
2018	LAN	MLB	27	604	103	34.9	.345	0.9	SS(81): 3.7, CF(50): -4.5	2.7
2019	LAN	MLB	28	546	105	24.6	.332	0.5	2B 0, LF 2	2.4

Chris Taylor, continued

Batted Ball Distribution

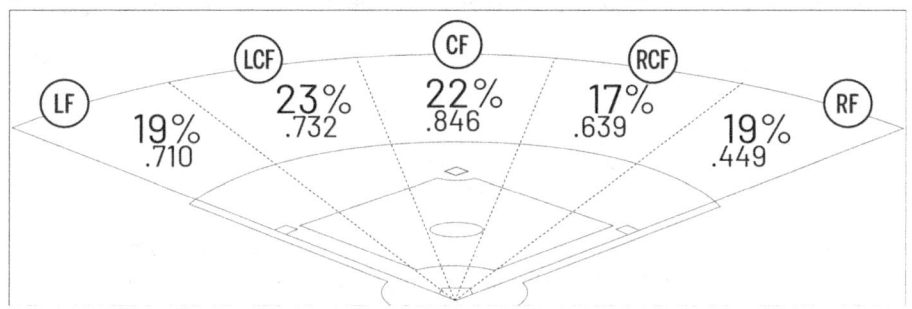

Strike Zone vs LHP

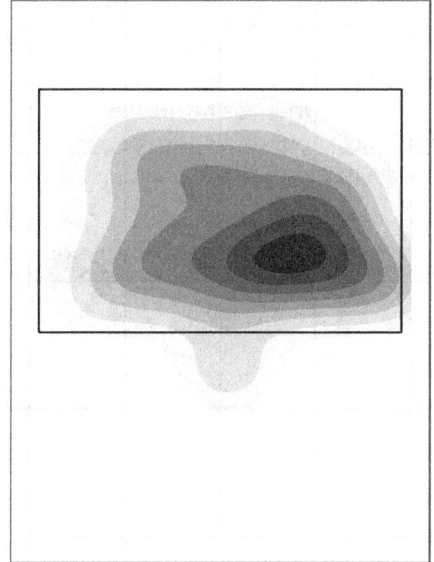

Strike Zone vs RHP

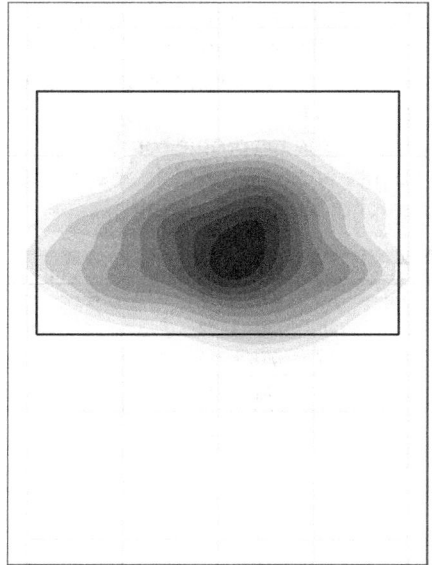

Justin Turner 3B

Born: 11/23/84 Age: 34 Bats: R Throws: R
Height: 5'11" Weight: 205 Origin: Round 7, 2006 Draft (#204 overall)

YEAR	TEAM	LVL	AGE	PA	R	2B	3B	HR	RBI	BB	K	SB	CS	AVG/OBP/SLG
2016	LAN	MLB	31	622	79	34	3	27	90	48	107	4	1	.275/.339/.493
2017	LAN	MLB	32	543	72	32	0	21	71	59	56	7	1	.322/.415/.530
2018	LAN	MLB	33	426	62	31	1	14	52	47	54	2	1	.312/.406/.518
2019	LAN	MLB	34	586	74	36	2	19	77	56	89	5	1	.293/.378/.483

Breakout: 1% Improve: 32% Collapse: 19% Attrition: 5% MLB: 97%
Comparables: George Brett, Aramis Ramirez, Chipper Jones

If you ever wondered what might happen if a radioactive George Brett bit Gritty (and of course you have), you'd probably wind up with something like Turner, who continued his ascent up the list of the 30-40 biggest regrets for Mets fans with yet another strong season at the plate. For many hitters, a broken wrist suffered in Spring Training might be a decent excuse for a down year, especially when nicks to the shoulder, hip and groin all conspired to hold him down throughout the season's first half. Not for Turner, who rebounded with a scorching hot second-half line of .356/.447/.619. The ginger wonder was also a strong defender at the hot corner, a feat he hadn't accomplished since the 2014 season, his first in Tinseltown. This bodes well for Turner, as he hurtles into his mid-30s, and his profile combining minuscule strikeout totals with decent patience and a little pop is one that should age better than the opening metaphor for this comment.

YEAR	TEAM	LVL	AGE	PA	DRC+	VORP	BABIP	BRR	FRAA	WARP
2016	LAN	MLB	31	622	122	49.2	.293	-1.7	3B(144): -4.8, 1B(1): 0.0	3.2
2017	LAN	MLB	32	543	149	63.8	.326	-3.2	3B(121): -5.5	4.4
2018	LAN	MLB	33	426	146	43.8	.334	0.3	3B(96): 11.1	5.1
2019	LAN	MLB	34	586	133	36.8	.320	-0.6	3B 1	3.8

Justin Turner, continued

Batted Ball Distribution

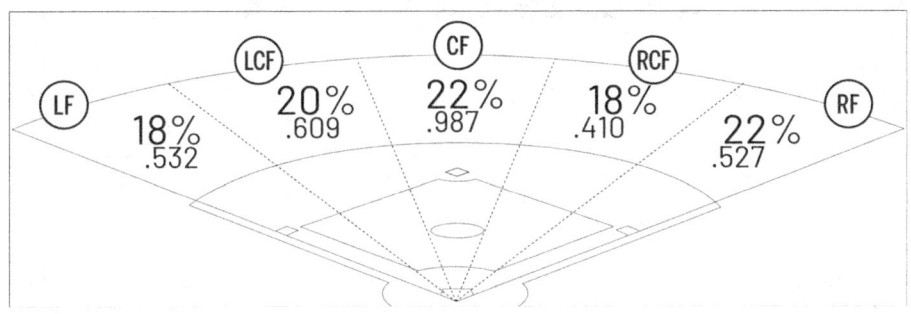

Strike Zone vs LHP

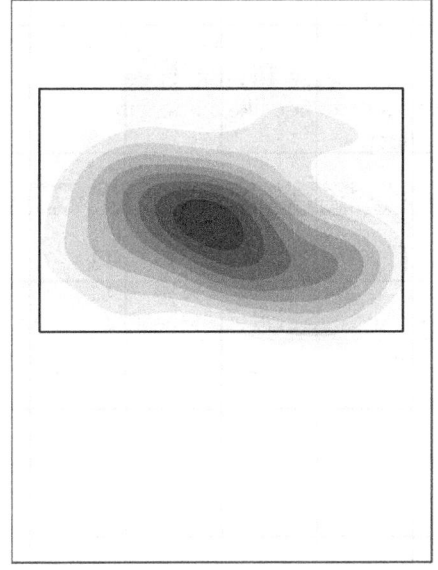

Strike Zone vs RHP

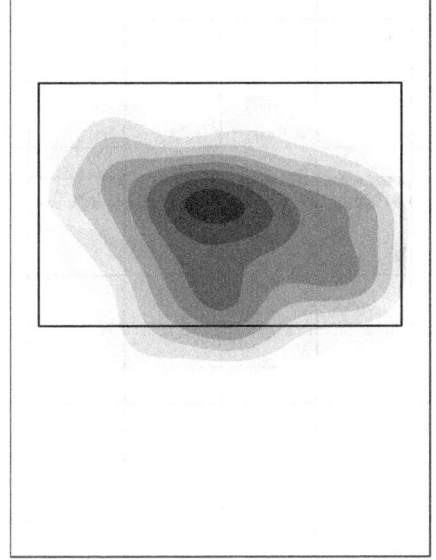

Scott Alexander LHP

Born: 07/10/89   Age: 29   Bats: L   Throws: L
Height: 6'2"   Weight: 190   Origin: Round 6, 2010 Draft (#179 overall)

YEAR	TEAM	LVL	AGE	W	L	SV	G	GS	IP	H	HR	BB/9	K/9	K	GB%	BABIP
2016	OMA	AAA	26	2	0	1	22	0	30	32	2	3.0	7.2	24	67%	.323
2016	KCA	MLB	26	0	0	0	17	0	19	24	1	3.3	7.6	16	69%	.383
2017	KCA	MLB	27	5	4	4	58	0	69	62	3	3.7	7.7	59	73%	.306
2018	LAN	MLB	28	2	1	3	73	1	66	57	4	3.7	7.6	56	72%	.296
2019	LAN	MLB	29	2	2	2	38	0	40	37	4	3.8	8.0	36	62%	.294

Breakout: 33%   Improve: 49%   Collapse: 27%   Attrition: 25%   MLB: 88%
Comparables: Sam Dyson, Jeremy Jeffress, Matt Grace

Acquired by the Dodgers in a January three-team trade, Alexander wore out the path between the bullpen and the mound this season, pitching in almost half of all games for his new club; His 73 appearances ranked eighth in the National League. The southpaw tinkers with four pitches, but really he throws only one, a sinker he deploys roughly 85 percent of the time to coax an elite rate of ground balls. Despite handling right-handed bats in Kansas City, Alexander's reverse splits backed up a bit in 2018, and he still probably walks a few more guys than you'd prefer from a late-inning option. Nevertheless, with another year to go before arbitration, the Dodgers hope Alexander can age like a fine wine, a fitting desire for the Sonoma State University product.

YEAR	TEAM	LVL	AGE	WHIP	ERA	DRA	WARP	MPH	FB%	WHF	CSP
2016	OMA	AAA	26	1.40	3.00	3.47	0.5				
2016	KCA	MLB	26	1.63	3.32	5.33	-0.1	94.1	72.2	13.3	45.6
2017	KCA	MLB	27	1.30	2.48	4.64	0.4	95.0	93.9	14.3	45.6
2018	LAN	MLB	28	1.27	3.68	5.33	-0.3	95.1	85.6	12.4	46.5
2019	LAN	MLB	29	1.34	3.69	4.06	0.3	94.3	87.8	13.3	46

Scott Alexander, continued

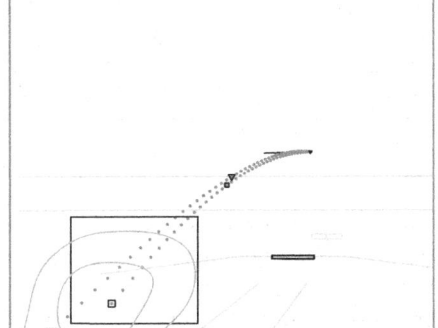
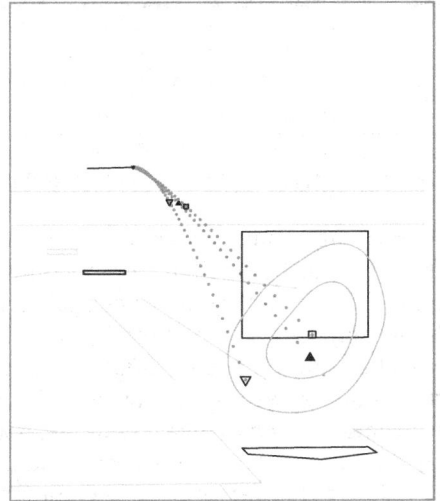

Type	Frequency	Velocity	H Movement	V Movement
● Fastball	1.8%	92.7 [101]	11.6 [77]	-18.2 [92]
□ Sinker	83.8%	93.8 [106]	12.6 [100]	-23.8 [89]
+ Cutter				
▲ Changeup	3.5%	87.1 [107]	13.3 [89]	-29.4 [94]
× Splitter				
▽ Slider	10.9%	85.8 [106]	-2.1 [88]	-34.8 [95]
◇ Curveball				
⊕ Slow Curveball				
✳ Knuckleball				
▼ Screwball				

Pedro Baez RHP

Born: 03/11/88   Age: 31   Bats: R   Throws: R
Height: 6'0"   Weight: 230   Origin: International Free Agent, 2007

YEAR	TEAM	LVL	AGE	W	L	SV	G	GS	IP	H	HR	BB/9	K/9	K	GB%	BABIP
2016	LAN	MLB	28	3	2	0	73	0	74	52	11	2.7	10.1	83	44%	.233
2017	LAN	MLB	29	3	6	0	66	0	64	56	9	4.1	9.0	64	35%	.267
2018	LAN	MLB	30	4	3	0	55	0	56^1	46	4	3.7	9.9	62	38%	.286
2019	LAN	MLB	31	3	3	0	53	0	55	51	9	3.5	9.4	58	40%	.284

Breakout: 33%   Improve: 48%   Collapse: 26%   Attrition: 16%   MLB: 94%
Comparables: Matt Bush, Santiago Casilla, Brad Brach

As Mick Jagger famously belted, "Time is on my side, yes it is". It's fair to say that this lyric is likely crocheted onto a throw pillow in Baez's living room, as the hard-throwing righty was once again among the league's most deliberate hurlers on the bump. But really, what is time? People used to think that time was the same everywhere. But then Einstein got involved, and we...observer. It turns out that we, as humans, perceive time differently and relatively to the instruments used to measure time. So what if time is just an agreed upon social construct? And if that's the case, is Baez really that painfully slow, or are the reactions to his pace more of a commentary on where we're at as a society and our ever-shrinking attention spans? Either way, Baez is pitching high-leverage innings again, and is acquitting himself well. At least there's that.

YEAR	TEAM	LVL	AGE	WHIP	ERA	DRA	WARP	MPH	FB%	WHF	CSP
2016	LAN	MLB	28	1.00	3.04	3.18	1.5	99.2	74.8	15.7	46.5
2017	LAN	MLB	29	1.33	2.95	4.81	0.3	98.6	72.7	17	44.8
2018	LAN	MLB	30	1.22	2.88	3.35	1.0	97.7	62.8	16.1	44
2019	LAN	MLB	31	1.29	4.39	4.64	0.1	97.6	69.2	16.2	44.6

Pedro Baez, continued

Pitch Shape vs LHH

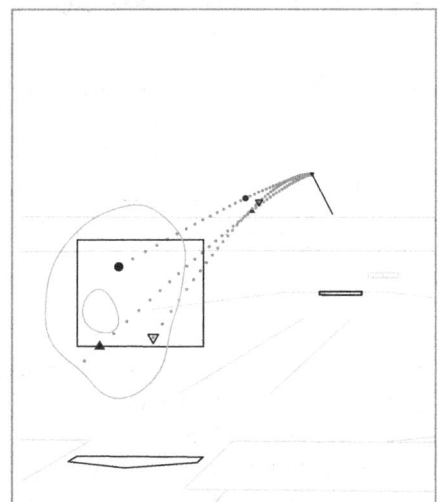

Pitch Shape vs RHH

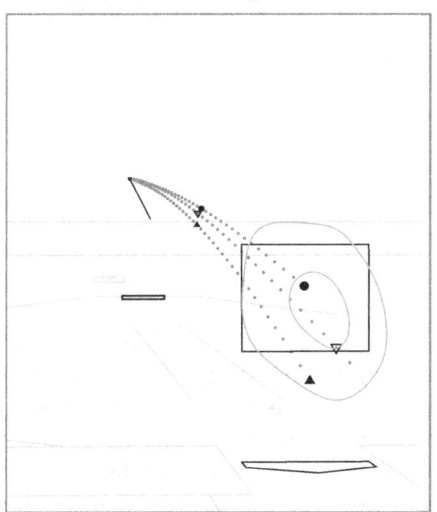

Type	Frequency	Velocity	H Movement	V Movement
● Fastball	61.5%	96.5 [113]	-6.9 [99]	-11.4 [114]
☐ Sinker	1.3%	96.2 [119]	-11.9 [106]	-14.2 [120]
+ Cutter				
▲ Changeup	14.7%	87.3 [108]	-10.4 [104]	-21.6 [117]
✕ Splitter				
▽ Slider	22.6%	88.5 [118]	2.1 [88]	-26 [121]
◇ Curveball				
⊕ Slow Curveball				
✳ Knuckleball				
▼ Screwball				

Walker Buehler RHP

Born: 07/28/94 Age: 24 Bats: R Throws: R
Height: 6'2" Weight: 175 Origin: Round 1, 2015 Draft (#24 overall)

YEAR	TEAM	LVL	AGE	W	L	SV	G	GS	IP	H	HR	BB/9	K/9	K	GB%	BABIP
2017	RCU	A+	22	0	0	0	5	5	16^1	8	0	2.8	14.9	27	57%	.267
2017	TUL	AA	22	2	2	0	11	11	49	40	5	2.8	11.8	64	52%	.315
2017	OKL	AAA	22	1	1	1	12	3	23^1	19	1	4.2	13.1	34	62%	.333
2017	LAN	MLB	22	1	0	0	8	0	9^1	11	2	7.7	11.6	12	67%	.409
2018	OKL	AAA	23	1	0	0	3	3	13	10	0	2.8	11.1	16	61%	.303
2018	LAN	MLB	23	8	5	0	24	23	137^1	95	12	2.4	9.9	151	50%	.248
2019	LAN	MLB	24	11	8	0	26	26	156	130	18	3.5	10.1	175	49%	.285

Breakout: 22% Improve: 61% Collapse: 6% Attrition: 10% MLB: 95%
Comparables: Luis Severino, Lance McCullers, Carlos Martinez

At the risk of running a reference into the ground, Buehler is very popular. The sportos, motorheads, geeks, wastoids, dweebies—they all adore him. They think he's a righteous dude. They're not wrong. Coming off an especially bitter cup of coffee in his first stint with the team down the stretch of 2017, Buehler was finally inserted into the rotation this season, and he didn't disappoint. Armed with a deep five-pitch mix including a heater that can run into triple digits, the rookie tossed 177 innings in 2018, including the playoffs—by far his heaviest workload as a professional. The stuff didn't fade, as the former Vanderbilt star finished strong, punching out 29 batters in 23.1 playoff innings, including seven dazzling and scoreless innings in Game 3 of the World Series. And after showing 80-grade proclivity for dropping public expletives during candid celebratory moments, it's safe to say that's Walker "F-ing" Buehler to you.

YEAR	TEAM	LVL	AGE	WHIP	ERA	DRA	WARP	MPH	FB%	WHF	CSP
2017	RCU	A+	22	0.80	1.10	1.77	0.7				
2017	TUL	AA	22	1.12	3.49	2.75	1.4				
2017	OKL	AAA	22	1.29	4.63	3.03	0.6				
2017	LAN	MLB	22	2.04	7.71	4.10	0.1	99.5	69.8	11.5	47.9
2018	OKL	AAA	23	1.08	2.08	3.07	0.4				
2018	LAN	MLB	23	0.96	2.62	3.21	3.3	98.2	59.6	12.6	49.5
2019	LAN	MLB	24	1.20	3.63	3.96	2.0	98.1	62.1	12.9	50.3

Walker Buehler, continued

Pitch Shape vs LHH

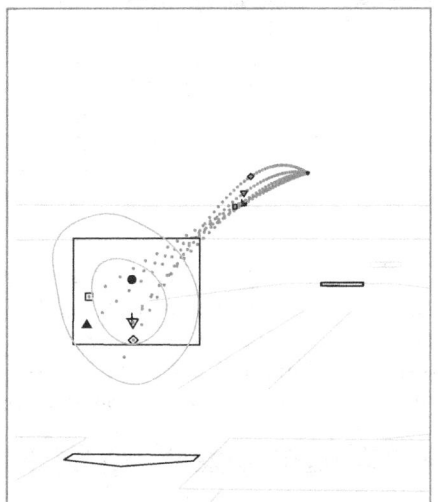

Pitch Shape vs RHH

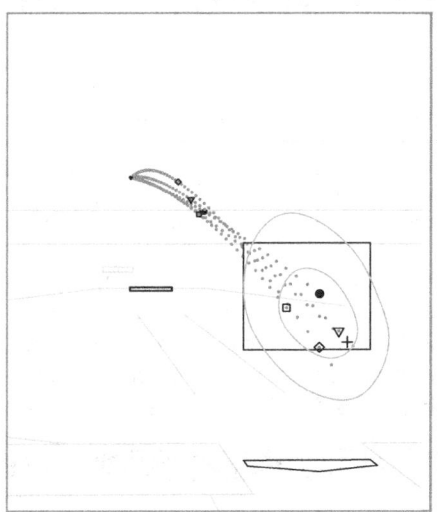

Type	Frequency	Velocity	H Movement	V Movement
● Fastball	41.5%	96.7 [113]	-3.1 [116]	-10.3 [117]
□ Sinker	18.1%	96.4 [120]	-10.7 [116]	-13.8 [121]
+ Cutter	12.0%	91.7 [117]	5.8 [123]	-22.6 [105]
▲ Changeup	3.7%	90.4 [120]	-10.5 [104]	-21.1 [118]
✕ Splitter				
▽ Slider	11.2%	86.7 [110]	8.6 [116]	-32.6 [101]
◇ Curveball	13.5%	80.5 [108]	7.7 [99]	-51.6 [92]
⊕ Slow Curveball				
✱ Knuckleball				
▼ Screwball				

Tony Cingrani LHP
Born: 07/05/89 Age: 29 Bats: L Throws: L
Height: 6'4" Weight: 214 Origin: Round 3, 2011 Draft (#114 overall)

YEAR	TEAM	LVL	AGE	W	L	SV	G	GS	IP	H	HR	BB/9	K/9	K	GB%	BABIP
2016	CIN	MLB	26	2	5	17	65	0	63	54	5	5.3	7.0	49	48%	.277
2017	CIN	MLB	27	0	0	0	25	0	23^1	25	9	2.3	9.3	24	43%	.271
2017	LAN	MLB	27	0	0	0	22	0	19^1	15	1	2.8	13.0	28	42%	.333
2018	LAN	MLB	28	1	2	0	30	0	22^2	19	2	2.4	14.3	36	54%	.354
2019	LAN	MLB	29	2	2	0	34	0	35	28	3	3.9	11.3	45	47%	.293

Breakout: 30%   Improve: 48%   Collapse: 23%   Attrition: 11%   MLB: 89%
Comparables: David Hernandez, Dennys Reyes, Ken Howell

If Cingrani's season were a car, it wouldn't get very good gas mileage on account of all the starts and stops. The southpaw spent more time on the DL than off in 2018, which is a shame, as a career-high slider usage led to his best strikeout rate since an abbreviated 2012 cup of coffee. In the land of Priuses and Teslas, here's hoping Cingrani can find something a little more reliable moving forward.

YEAR	TEAM	LVL	AGE	WHIP	ERA	DRA	WARP	MPH	FB%	WHF	CSP
2016	CIN	MLB	26	1.44	4.14	6.57	-1.2	96.7	87.4	9.6	47.6
2017	CIN	MLB	27	1.33	5.40	6.06	-0.2	95.9	90	14	52.4
2017	LAN	MLB	27	1.09	2.79	2.70	0.5	96.2	72	15.7	40.9
2018	LAN	MLB	28	1.10	4.76	3.90	0.3	95.6	78	16.1	45.4
2019	LAN	MLB	29	1.21	3.07	3.55	0.5	95.5	83	13	46.4

Tony Cingrani, continued

Pitch Shape vs LHH

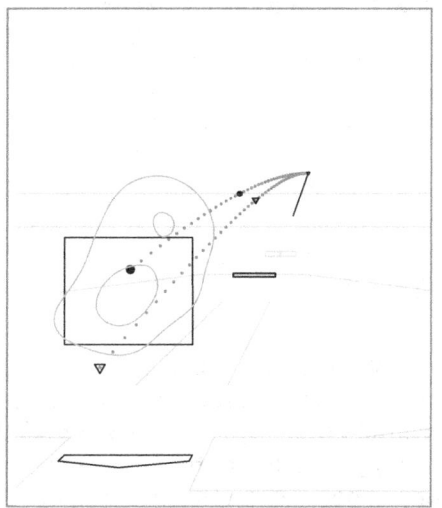

Pitch Shape vs RHH

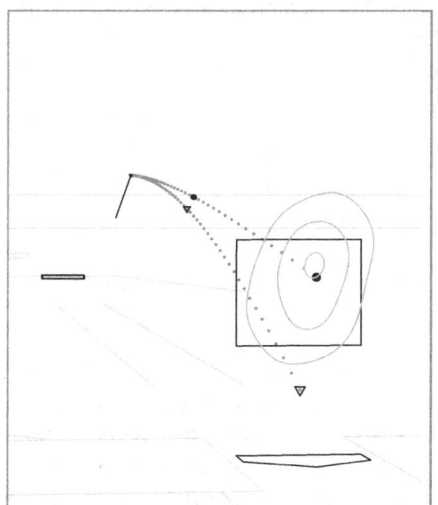

Type	Frequency	Velocity	H Movement	V Movement
● Fastball	78.0%	94.3 [106]	4.8 [109]	-16 [99]
☐ Sinker				
+ Cutter				
▲ Changeup	2.7%	90.1 [119]	7.7 [119]	-23.2 [112]
✕ Splitter				
▽ Slider	19.4%	83.1 [94]	-8.3 [115]	-32.3 [102]
◇ Curveball				
⊕ Slow Curveball				
✱ Knuckleball				
▼ Screwball				

Caleb Ferguson LHP
Born: 07/02/96   Age: 22   Bats: R   Throws: L
Height: 6'3"   Weight: 215   Origin: Round 38, 2014 Draft (#1149 overall)

YEAR	TEAM	LVL	AGE	W	L	SV	G	GS	IP	H	HR	BB/9	K/9	K	GB%	BABIP
2016	DOD	RK	19	1	0	0	2	0	6	4	0	0.0	16.5	11	38%	.308
2016	OGD	RK	19	1	0	0	2	2	10	4	0	1.8	9.9	11	67%	.167
2016	GRL	A	19	1	4	0	10	10	50^1	49	3	0.5	7.3	41	60%	.309
2017	RCU	A+	20	9	4	0	25	24	122^1	113	6	4.0	10.3	140	46%	.335
2018	TUL	AA	21	3	0	0	8	8	39	31	2	2.3	9.2	40	42%	.284
2018	OKL	AAA	21	0	0	0	2	2	8	6	0	7.9	13.5	12	21%	.316
2018	LAN	MLB	21	7	2	2	29	3	49	43	8	2.2	10.8	59	47%	.292
2019	*LAN*	*MLB*	*22*	*3*	*2*	*0*	*37*	*3*	*49^2*	*44*	*6*	*3.0*	*9.6*	*53*	*45%*	*.292*

Breakout: 22%   Improve: 31%   Collapse: 9%   Attrition: 25%   MLB: 51%
Comparables: Tyler Skaggs, Lucas Giolito, Francis Martes

While it surely stung to be left off the 25-man World Series roster, it's hard to call the 2018 season anything but a success for Ferguson, who started the campaign as a Double-A hurler, barely old enough to legally order a beer. Installed as a full-time, late-inning option in late June, the southpaw rode a fastball touching 97 mph and a biting curve to gaudy strikeout numbers. Ferguson's first foray into the postseason resulted in retiring nine of the 10 batters he faced, punching out three in three innings of work. The former 38th-round pick's future role as a big leaguer will likely be determined by curbing bouts of shaky control, and his changeup, which is still a work in progress.

YEAR	TEAM	LVL	AGE	WHIP	ERA	DRA	WARP	MPH	FB%	WHF	CSP
2016	DOD	RK	19	0.67	1.50	1.30	0.3				
2016	OGD	RK	19	0.60	0.90	3.15	0.3				
2016	GRL	A	19	1.03	2.68	4.03	0.6				
2017	RCU	A+	20	1.37	2.87	4.03	1.8				
2018	TUL	AA	21	1.05	1.38	4.07	0.6				
2018	OKL	AAA	21	1.62	2.25	3.79	0.2				
2018	LAN	MLB	21	1.12	3.49	3.17	1.0	96.1	71.9	12.5	54.7
2019	*LAN*	*MLB*	*22*	*1.22*	*3.63*	*4.01*	*0.5*	*96.1*	*75*	*13.1*	*57*

Caleb Ferguson, continued

Pitch Shape vs LHH

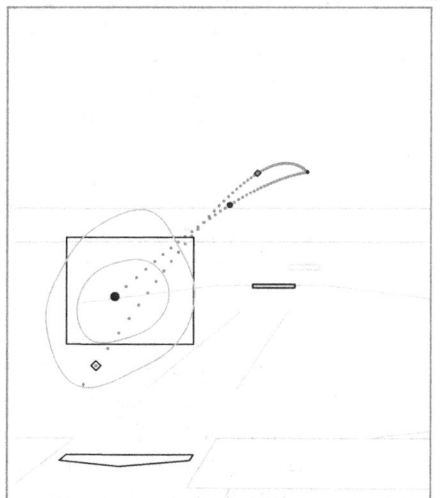

Pitch Shape vs RHH

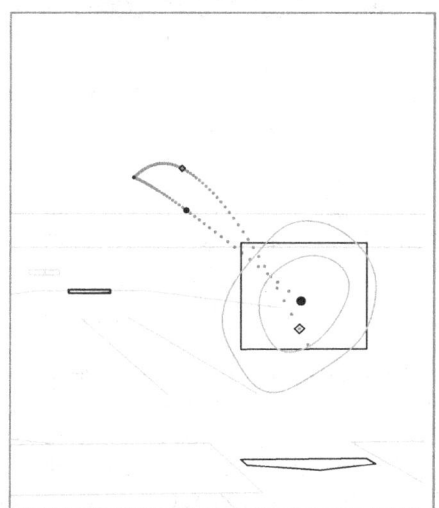

Type	Frequency	Velocity	H Movement	V Movement
● Fastball	71.9%	94.2 [105]	8.7 [91]	-13.1 [108]
☐ Sinker				
+ Cutter				
▲ Changeup	3.1%	85.2 [100]	7.8 [118]	-21.4 [118]
✕ Splitter				
▽ Slider	0.1%	82.5 [91]	-4.1 [97]	-34.9 [94]
◇ Curveball	24.8%	75.9 [91]	-6 [92]	-58.9 [76]
✢ Slow Curveball				
✳ Knuckleball				
▼ Screwball				

Dylan Floro RHP
Born: 12/27/90 Age: 28 Bats: L Throws: R
Height: 6'2" Weight: 205 Origin: Round 13, 2012 Draft (#422 overall)

YEAR	TEAM	LVL	AGE	W	L	SV	G	GS	IP	H	HR	BB/9	K/9	K	GB%	BABIP
2016	TBA	MLB	25	0	1	0	12	0	15	23	0	3.0	8.4	14	55%	.434
2016	DUR	AAA	25	1	2	7	32	0	50	53	6	1.6	7.2	40	56%	.313
2017	CHN	MLB	26	0	0	0	3	0	9^2	15	2	1.9	5.6	6	53%	.382
2017	IOW	AAA	26	3	2	1	25	2	48^2	54	9	1.5	4.8	26	63%	.274
2017	OKL	AAA	26	0	1	1	8	0	11^1	18	0	2.4	9.5	12	58%	.474
2018	CIN	MLB	27	3	2	0	25	0	36^1	39	2	3.0	6.7	27	57%	.314
2018	LAN	MLB	27	3	1	0	29	0	27^2	18	1	3.6	10.1	31	55%	.250
2019	LAN	MLB	28	2	2	0	38	0	40	40	5	3.2	8.2	37	53%	.302

Breakout: 13% Improve: 24% Collapse: 18% Attrition: 20% MLB: 54%
Comparables: Matt Grace, Brian Flynn, Tyler Olson

The journeyman right-hander went west in July, marking his fourth club in a two-year span. The move paid off handsomely, as Floro's ERA sparkled for the Dodgers, holding opposition hitters to a .522 OPS in the second half and punching out over 10 batters per nine, ultimately emerging as one of the team's lone trusted options out of the pen in late-inning situations. He also won the coveted Full Vogelsong Pitcher of the Year award, which is nice. However, the real tragedy of Floro's season was that the Dodgers traded Brandon McCarthy, depriving Dave Roberts of the opportunity to replace Brandon with Dylan.

YEAR	TEAM	LVL	AGE	WHIP	ERA	DRA	WARP	MPH	FB%	WHF	CSP
2016	TBA	MLB	25	1.87	4.20	6.14	-0.2	95.1	73.8	10.2	49.9
2016	DUR	AAA	25	1.24	2.88	3.60	0.8				
2017	CHN	MLB	26	1.76	6.52	6.19	-0.1	93.0	67.7	9.8	54.8
2017	IOW	AAA	26	1.27	3.88	4.08	0.7				
2017	OKL	AAA	26	1.85	5.56	2.63	0.3				
2018	CIN	MLB	27	1.40	2.72	5.25	-0.1	94.7	62.4	9.8	48.1
2018	LAN	MLB	27	1.05	1.63	3.14	0.6	95.5	64.8	15.3	45
2019	LAN	MLB	28	1.37	4.01	4.31	0.2	94.3	65.4	11.8	50.5

Dylan Floro, continued

Pitch Shape vs LHH

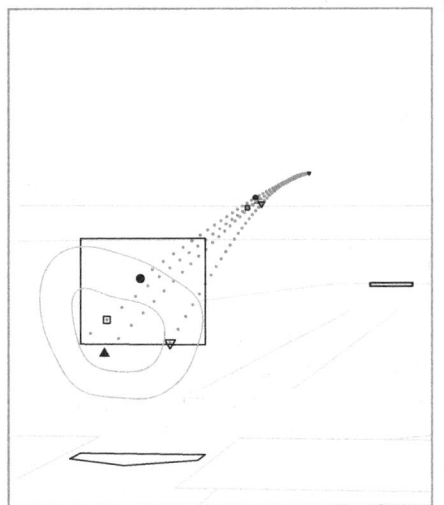

Pitch Shape vs RHH

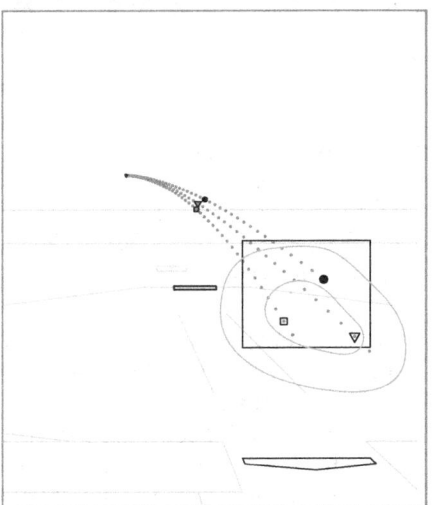

Type	Frequency	Velocity	H Movement	V Movement
● Fastball	12.4%	94.1 [105]	-8.5 [92]	-15 [102]
□ Sinker	51.0%	93.7 [106]	-14.4 [85]	-21.2 [97]
+ Cutter				
▲ Changeup	8.4%	86.5 [105]	-13.3 [89]	-30.3 [91]
× Splitter				
▽ Slider	28.2%	87.4 [113]	2.4 [89]	-27.2 [117]
◇ Curveball				
⊕ Slow Curveball				
✳ Knuckleball				
▼ Screwball				

Los Angeles Dodgers 2019

Donnie Hart   LHP

Born: 09/06/90   Age: 28   Bats: L   Throws: L
Height: 5'11"   Weight: 180   Origin: Round 27, 2013 Draft (#819 overall)

YEAR	TEAM	LVL	AGE	W	L	SV	G	GS	IP	H	HR	BB/9	K/9	K	GB%	BABIP
2016	BOW	AA	25	3	1	4	40	0	46^1	41	1	1.4	9.7	50	50%	.325
2016	BAL	MLB	25	0	0	0	22	0	18^1	12	1	2.9	5.9	12	60%	.212
2017	NOR	AAA	26	1	0	0	13	0	15^1	17	1	1.2	11.7	20	55%	.390
2017	BAL	MLB	26	2	0	0	51	0	43^2	48	5	2.7	6.0	29	54%	.309
2018	NOR	AAA	27	3	2	6	32	3	41	42	1	2.2	9.9	45	62%	.360
2018	BAL	MLB	27	0	0	0	20	0	19^1	31	2	5.6	6.1	13	46%	.403
2019	*LAN*	*MLB*	*28*	*1*	*1*	*0*	*19*	*0*	*20^1*	*21*	*3*	*3.3*	*7.7*	*17*	*50%*	*.300*

Breakout: 20%   Improve: 34%   Collapse: 24%   Attrition: 27%   MLB: 66%
Comparables: Bryan Morris, Brian Wolfe, Royce Ring

For many teams, a 27th-round draft pick making it to the major leagues would be a story of inspiration and triumph against adversity. Sadly, by his third turn in the majors, Hart's strong minor league numbers have been eclipsed by major-league struggles. On September 26th, in a game against the Red Sox, the Orioles decided to try out the newfangled "Opener" strategy popularized by the Rays. Why let the inconsequential detail that the Rays 'pen was top-five in the league and the Orioles' was bottom-five stop them? The O's-pener made it all of 20 pitches, allowing two runs and loading the bases again before being pulled for Hart, who promptly surrendered a bases-clearing double and inspired a spate of bad puns based on his last name on Twitter. Tom Petty was wrong; it's the punning that's the hardest part.

YEAR	TEAM	LVL	AGE	WHIP	ERA	DRA	WARP	MPH	FB%	WHF	CSP
2016	BOW	AA	25	1.04	2.72	2.48	1.2				
2016	BAL	MLB	25	0.98	0.49	4.64	0.1	89.7	46.1	9.7	45.4
2017	NOR	AAA	26	1.24	2.35	2.10	0.5				
2017	BAL	MLB	26	1.40	3.71	5.56	-0.2	88.8	48	10.7	39.4
2018	NOR	AAA	27	1.27	2.41	3.16	1.0				
2018	BAL	MLB	27	2.22	5.59	7.84	-0.6	89.3	56.5	9.2	50.6
2019	*LAN*	*MLB*	*28*	*1.40*	*4.28*	*4.54*	*0.1*	*88.6*	*50.9*	*10.1*	*45.8*

Donnie Hart, continued

Pitch Shape vs LHH

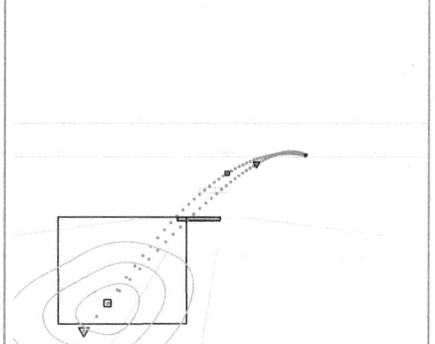

Pitch Shape vs RHH

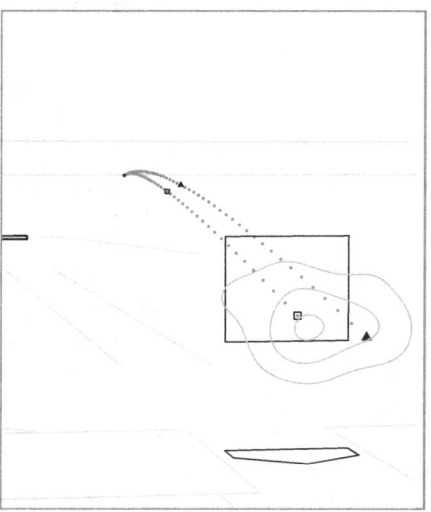

Type	Frequency	Velocity	H Movement	V Movement
● Fastball				
☐ Sinker	56.5%	88.2 [79]	15.9 [73]	-33.1 [58]
+ Cutter				
▲ Changeup	11.0%	81 [83]	15.3 [79]	-42.6 [55]
✕ Splitter				
▽ Slider	32.5%	76.5 [64]	-9.1 [118]	-43 [70]
◇ Curveball				
⊕ Slow Curveball				
✳ Knuckleball				
▼ Screwball				

Los Angeles Dodgers 2019

Rich Hill LHP
Born: 03/11/80   Age: 39   Bats: L   Throws: L
Height: 6'5"   Weight: 220   Origin: Round 4, 2002 Draft (#112 overall)

YEAR	TEAM	LVL	AGE	W	L	SV	G	GS	IP	H	HR	BB/9	K/9	K	GB%	BABIP
2016	OAK	MLB	36	9	3	0	14	14	76	55	2	3.3	10.7	90	51%	.290
2016	LAN	MLB	36	3	2	0	6	6	34^1	22	2	1.3	10.2	39	38%	.244
2017	LAN	MLB	37	12	8	0	25	25	135^2	99	18	3.3	11.0	166	39%	.261
2018	LAN	MLB	38	11	5	0	25	24	132^2	108	20	2.8	10.2	150	40%	.268
2019	LAN	MLB	39	10	6	0	23	23	138	117	17	2.8	9.9	152	42%	.286

Breakout: 11%   Improve: 39%   Collapse: 13%   Attrition: 5%   MLB: 77%
Comparables: Roger Clemens, Nolan Ryan, Allie Reynolds

In 2017, MLB started promoting the Player's Weekend, a stretch of games where teams could wear fun uniforms (read: sell more merch) and players could flaunt their personalities by donning wacky monikers on the backs of their jerseys. If it sounds like a practice that a 38-year-old veteran hurler would find immature or distasteful, well, you'd be wrong. On August 24, "D. Mountain" took the bump for the Dodgers, and dominated a hapless Padres lineup, tossing a perfect game through four innings. Just when the possibility of Hill sending his nicknamed jersey to Cooperstown flickered in the distance, Hunter Renfroe doubled, ruining it for everyone. In the end, Hill punched out eight batters in six shutout innings, a vintage performance for the reinvented southpaw. The problem for Hill was that these outings were flanked by more clunkers—he allowed at least four earned runs in eight starts during 2018, compared to just three in 2017. As he enters his age-39 season, and the last season of his three-year contract, he'll be looking to recapture the ability to consistently baffle hitters with a steady diet of Uncle Charlies, and he'll do so in style.

YEAR	TEAM	LVL	AGE	WHIP	ERA	DRA	WARP	MPH	FB%	WHF	CSP
2016	OAK	MLB	36	1.09	2.25	2.75	2.3	93.0	46.6	12.1	50.9
2016	LAN	MLB	36	0.79	1.83	2.89	1.0	92.2	48.3	11.6	50.9
2017	LAN	MLB	37	1.09	3.32	3.35	3.4	90.7	54.8	12.7	49.2
2018	LAN	MLB	38	1.12	3.66	3.92	2.1	91.2	58.8	11.6	54.5
2019	LAN	MLB	39	1.15	3.55	3.86	1.9	89.8	53.2	11.7	50.3

Rich Hill, continued

Pitch Shape vs LHH

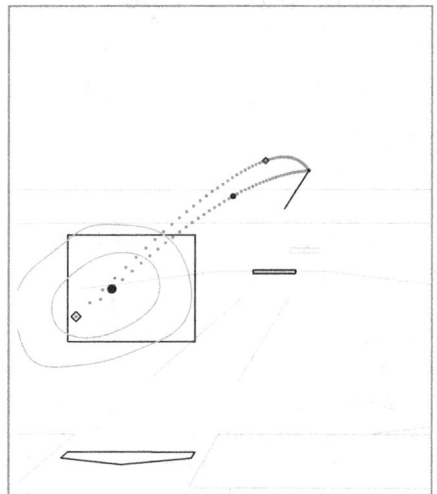

Pitch Shape vs RHH

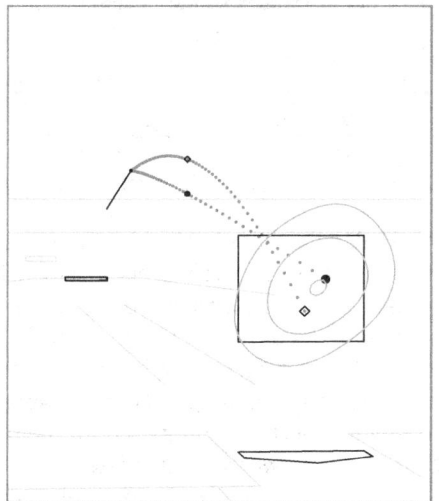

Type	Frequency	Velocity	H Movement	V Movement
● Fastball	57.7%	89.8 [91]	9.5 [87]	-15 [102]
☐ Sinker	1.1%	86.7 [71]	15.8 [73]	-25.6 [83]
+ Cutter	0.5%	85.4 [80]	-0.2 [90]	-25 [95]
▲ Changeup	0.8%	84.9 [98]	14.1 [85]	-27.1 [101]
✕ Splitter				
▽ Slider	0.3%	78.2 [72]	-8.1 [114]	-46 [61]
◇ Curveball	39.6%	74.8 [86]	-15.4 [132]	-55.8 [82]
⊕ Slow Curveball	0.0%	67.6 [100]	-15.9 [113]	-64.7 [102]
✳ Knuckleball				
▼ Screwball				

Kenley Jansen RHP

Born: 09/30/87 Age: 31 Bats: B Throws: R
Height: 6'5" Weight: 275 Origin: International Free Agent, 2004

YEAR	TEAM	LVL	AGE	W	L	SV	G	GS	IP	H	HR	BB/9	K/9	K	GB%	BABIP
2016	LAN	MLB	28	3	2	47	71	0	68²	35	4	1.4	13.6	104	33%	.238
2017	LAN	MLB	29	5	0	41	65	0	68¹	44	5	0.9	14.4	109	40%	.291
2018	LAN	MLB	30	1	5	38	69	0	71²	54	13	2.1	10.3	82	36%	.234
2019	LAN	MLB	31	3	2	38	53	0	55	47	8	2.5	10.7	66	37%	.287

Breakout: 33% Improve: 44% Collapse: 33% Attrition: 11% MLB: 95%
Comparables: Billy Wagner, David Robertson, Brad Lidge

It wasn't a banner year for the Dodger closer, and it speaks to Jansen's brilliance that such a comment is even possible. The Curacao native's River-ian cutter remained potent, with eye-popping vertical and horizontal movement, once again ranking as one of the nastiest, liveliest pitches in the game. Having said that, Jansen started slow, barely touching 90 on the gun with an ERA approaching 6.00 in April. Homers were also a sore spot, as he served up nearly three times as many dingers than the previous three seasons combined. But those on-field woes don't matter, not really at least. During a series in Colorado, Jansen was rushed to the hospital, his heart in atrial fibrillation, an ailment he dealt with twice before in his career. His heart was shocked back into normal rhythm, and he was given medication to abate the symptoms. Fortunately Jansen escaped without further damage, and offseason surgery was performed to rectify the condition. In a rare instance of literalism, sappy or not, Jansen pitched his heart out for his team.

YEAR	TEAM	LVL	AGE	WHIP	ERA	DRA	WARP	MPH	FB%	WHF	CSP
2016	LAN	MLB	28	0.67	1.83	1.93	2.4	96.6	93.8	18.8	53.3
2017	LAN	MLB	29	0.75	1.32	1.90	2.5	95.7	92	19.8	51.8
2018	LAN	MLB	30	0.99	3.01	2.56	2.0	94.7	94.2	14.6	49
2019	LAN	MLB	31	1.11	3.09	3.56	0.8	94.6	92.8	17.1	50.7

Kenley Jansen, continued

Pitch Shape vs LHH

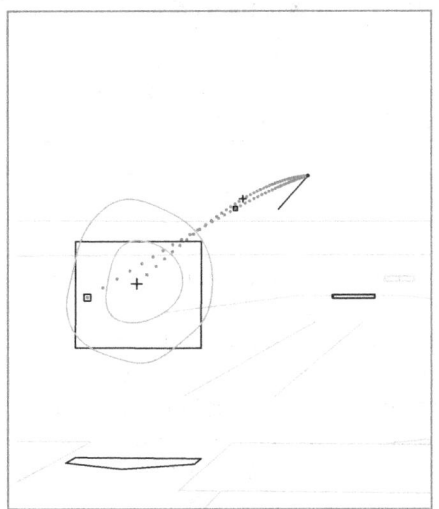

Pitch Shape vs RHH

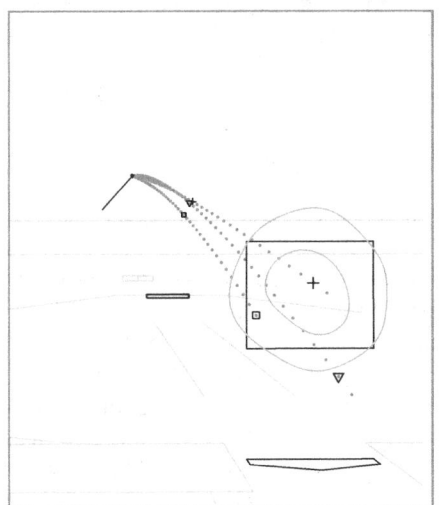

Type	Frequency	Velocity	H Movement	V Movement
● Fastball				
☐ Sinker	10.3%	94.3 [109]	-7.6 [142]	-12.1 [127]
+ Cutter	83.9%	92.7 [123]	6.8 [129]	-15.2 [134]
▲ Changeup				
✕ Splitter				
▽ Slider	5.8%	83.3 [95]	6 [105]	-38.7 [83]
◇ Curveball				
✦ Slow Curveball				
✳ Knuckleball				
▼ Screwball				

Los Angeles Dodgers 2019

Joe Kelly RHP
Born: 06/09/88 Age: 31 Bats: R Throws: R
Height: 6'1" Weight: 190 Origin: Round 3, 2009 Draft (#98 overall)

YEAR	TEAM	LVL	AGE	W	L	SV	G	GS	IP	H	HR	BB/9	K/9	K	GB%	BABIP
2016	PAW	AAA	28	1	1	2	17	4	35	29	1	1.5	11.8	46	57%	.341
2016	BOS	MLB	28	4	0	0	20	6	40	44	5	5.4	10.8	48	48%	.358
2017	BOS	MLB	29	4	1	0	54	0	58	42	3	4.2	8.1	52	51%	.252
2018	BOS	MLB	30	4	2	2	73	0	65²	57	4	4.4	9.3	68	49%	.301
2019	LAN	MLB	31	3	2	4	53	0	55	47	5	3.9	9.4	58	48%	.288

Breakout: 23%   Improve: 44%   Collapse: 21%   Attrition: 11%   MLB: 91%
Comparables: Ryan Dempster, Tyson Ross, Whitey Ford

It's been only four-and-a-half years since the Red Sox acquired Kelly and his Great Stuff™, but it feels like he's been pitching in Boston for two decades. Kelly has given Sox fans some memorable moments, from his infamous and ill-fated Cy Young prediction in 2015 to his clutch performance against Tyler Austin in Fight Night at Fenway and even more clutch exclamation point on the eighth inning of the World Series clincher. In 2018, he was occasionally brilliant and often frustrating, because this is Joe Kelly we're talking about. He was dominant in April, May and August. He was dominated in June, July and September. He almost got left off the postseason roster. Then he threw 11 1/3 innings of one-run ball in the playoffs, fanning 13 of the 44 batters he faced and earning the W in Game 4 of the World Series. Anyone who claims to know what the future holds in store for him is lying. He could be a dominant bridge to Kenley Jansen. He could be another big reliever bust. He'll probably end up being both somehow? All we know for sure is Joe Kelly still has Great Stuff™. He just doesn't always know how to use it.

YEAR	TEAM	LVL	AGE	WHIP	ERA	DRA	WARP	MPH	FB%	WHF	CSP
2016	PAW	AAA	28	1.00	1.54	2.06	1.2				
2016	BOS	MLB	28	1.70	5.18	5.10	0.0	100.4	65.6	11.4	43.8
2017	BOS	MLB	29	1.19	2.79	4.00	0.8	100.9	64.4	11.6	45.2
2018	BOS	MLB	30	1.36	4.39	4.56	0.3	100.2	55.4	11.4	45.8
2019	LAN	MLB	31	1.28	3.57	3.97	0.5	99.6	59.9	11.4	44.9

Joe Kelly, continued

Pitch Shape vs LHH

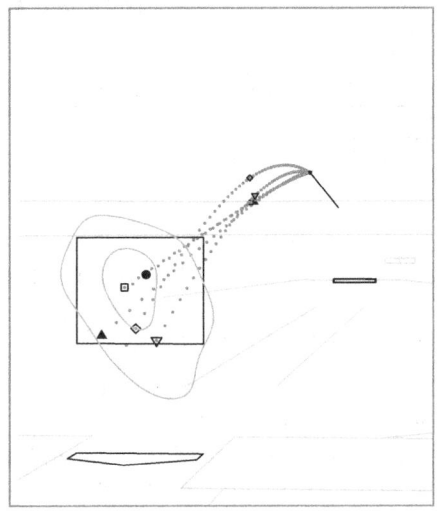

Pitch Shape vs RHH

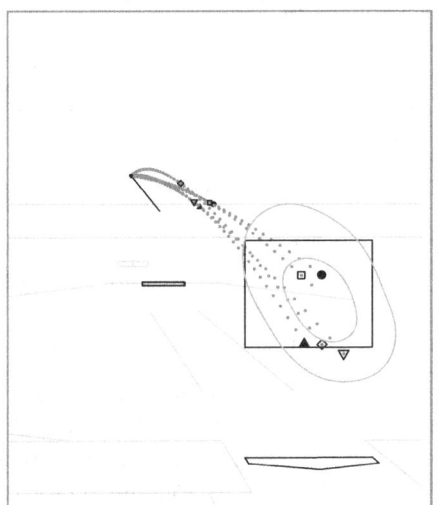

Type	Frequency	Velocity	H Movement	V Movement
● Fastball	47.6%	98.5 [119]	-7.6 [96]	-11.9 [112]
☐ Sinker	7.8%	97.9 [127]	-11.8 [107]	-14 [121]
+ Cutter				
▲ Changeup	10.9%	88 [111]	-14 [86]	-25.4 [106]
✕ Splitter				
▽ Slider	15.7%	88.1 [116]	5.9 [104]	-34.1 [97]
◇ Curveball	18.0%	84.5 [122]	8.4 [102]	-48.2 [100]
⊕ Slow Curveball				
✱ Knuckleball				
▼ Screwball				

Clayton Kershaw LHP

Born: 03/19/88 Age: 31 Bats: L Throws: L
Height: 6'4" Weight: 228 Origin: Round 1, 2006 Draft (#7 overall)

YEAR	TEAM	LVL	AGE	W	L	SV	G	GS	IP	H	HR	BB/9	K/9	K	GB%	BABIP
2016	LAN	MLB	28	12	4	0	21	21	149	97	8	0.7	10.4	172	51%	.254
2017	LAN	MLB	29	18	4	0	27	27	175	136	23	1.5	10.4	202	49%	.267
2018	LAN	MLB	30	9	5	0	26	26	161¹	139	17	1.6	8.6	155	50%	.274
2019	LAN	MLB	31	12	7	0	26	26	163	141	19	1.8	9.0	164	48%	.279

Breakout: 10% Improve: 31% Collapse: 31% Attrition: 7% MLB: 85%
Comparables: Roger Clemens, CC Sabathia, Brandon Webb

For the eighth time in his career, Kershaw pitched in the postseason, battling not only opposing lineups, but hot-take artists and straw men alike. And for the eighth time, he was mostly good, but also perhaps not at his peak. A weary fastball barely scraped 91 by October and yet again his bullpen crushed him.

Despite another dry final locker room, the former MVP and three-time Cy Young Award winner was still unquestionably great. For the 10th consecutive year, the ace posted an ERA under 3.00 and a WARP of at least 4.0. He's a surefire Hall-of-Famer. But for the fourth time in five seasons, Kershaw missed some time due to nagging injuries, and he lost nearly two ticks on his fastball, —further narrowing the velocity gap between the heater and his secondaries. He struck out fewer than a batter per inning for the first time since 2013, and with the emergence of Walker Buehler, the days of Kershaw being the most dominant force on his own staff might be numbered. The team effectively bought out his opt-out with a one-year contract extension, so at least we know that the greatest Dodger lefty since Koufax will call L.A.'s rotation home for another three seasons.

YEAR	TEAM	LVL	AGE	WHIP	ERA	DRA	WARP	MPH	FB%	WHF	CSP
2016	LAN	MLB	28	0.72	1.69	2.01	5.7	95.1	50.8	16.1	49.6
2017	LAN	MLB	29	0.95	2.31	2.24	6.5	94.3	47.8	15.3	46.5
2018	LAN	MLB	30	1.04	2.73	3.11	4.1	92.4	41.2	11.8	50.6
2019	LAN	MLB	31	1.03	3.26	3.54	2.9	92.9	45.4	13.9	48.7

Clayton Kershaw, continued

Pitch Shape vs LHH

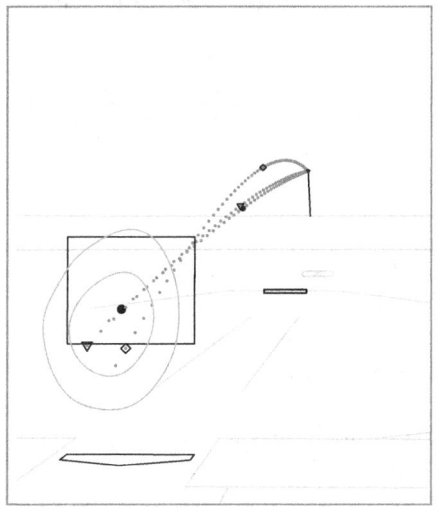

Pitch Shape vs RHH

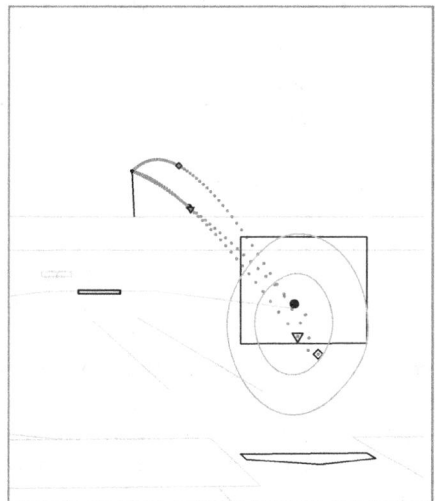

Type	Frequency	Velocity	H Movement	V Movement
● Fastball	41.0%	91.4 [96]	-0.2 [132]	-12.4 [111]
□ Sinker	0.2%	91.1 [93]	8.5 [134]	-14.1 [121]
+ Cutter				
▲ Changeup	0.4%	85.3 [100]	9 [112]	-18.5 [126]
× Splitter				
▽ Slider	41.9%	88.6 [118]	-3.4 [94]	-21 [135]
◇ Curveball	16.4%	73.4 [81]	-1.8 [74]	-61.1 [71]
⊕ Slow Curveball				
✳ Knuckleball				
▼ Screwball				

Los Angeles Dodgers 2019

Kenta Maeda RHP
Born: 04/11/88   Age: 31   Bats: R   Throws: R
Height: 6'1"   Weight: 175   Origin: International Free Agent, 2016

YEAR	TEAM	LVL	AGE	W	L	SV	G	GS	IP	H	HR	BB/9	K/9	K	GB%	BABIP
2016	LAN	MLB	28	16	11	0	32	32	175^2	150	20	2.6	9.2	179	45%	.283
2017	LAN	MLB	29	13	6	1	29	25	134^1	121	22	2.3	9.4	140	40%	.278
2018	LAN	MLB	30	8	10	2	39	20	125^1	115	13	3.1	11.0	153	42%	.321
2019	LAN	MLB	31	9	6	0	38	19	128	116	17	2.9	9.8	141	42%	.295

Breakout: 29%   Improve: 61%   Collapse: 22%   Attrition: 11%   MLB: 98%
Comparables: Zack Greinke, Cole Hamels, Bert Blyleven

In what has become an annual tradition, much like the Macy's Thanksgiving Day Parade or denouncements of "today's game" from the postseason commentators, the Dodgers shifted Maeda to the bullpen for the final stretch of the season. Maybe they did this to keep him fresh for a playoff run. Perhaps to accommodate the club's abundance of starters. Or, if you're a conspiracy theorist, you might note that the move worked with shocking convenience against several rounds of nearly-triggered contract bonus clauses. Regardless, the Japanese import rode a six-pitch mix to gaudy strikeout totals and a career-best swinging strike rate. For pitchers with at least 125 innings, his DRA ranked 13th-best, ahead of Luis Severino and Corey Kluber. But a hip strain cost Maeda a couple of weeks in June, once again stoking the concerns of fragility that dominated his posting process. It will be interesting to see how the yo-yoing affects Maeda's relationship with the team (if at all), as the parties are betrothed to one another through the 2023 season.

YEAR	TEAM	LVL	AGE	WHIP	ERA	DRA	WARP	MPH	FB%	WHF	CSP
2016	LAN	MLB	28	1.14	3.48	3.01	4.7	92.5	42.9	12.6	43.1
2017	LAN	MLB	29	1.15	4.22	3.53	3.0	93.3	43.4	13	47.1
2018	LAN	MLB	30	1.26	3.81	2.78	3.6	93.5	44.4	15.8	46.1
2019	LAN	MLB	31	1.23	3.71	4.05	1.5	92.3	43.3	13.8	45.4

Kenta Maeda, continued

Pitch Shape vs LHH

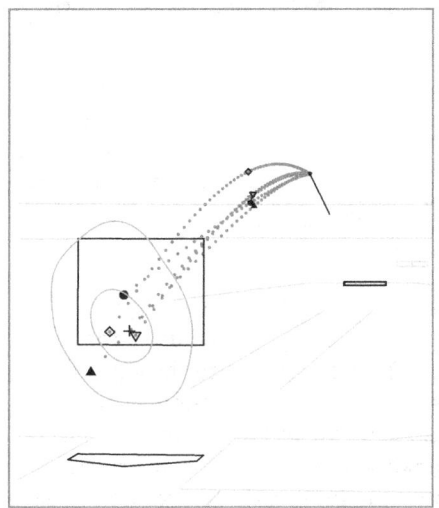

Pitch Shape vs RHH

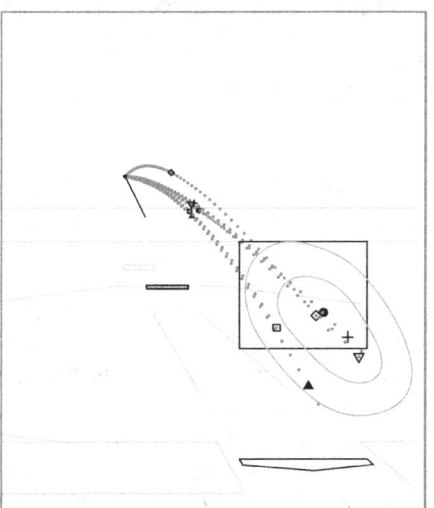

Type		Frequency	Velocity	H Movement	V Movement
●	Fastball	41.8%	92.5 [100]	-5.7 [105]	-14.1 [105]
□	Sinker	2.5%	91.2 [94]	-12.5 [101]	-20.3 [100]
+	Cutter	7.3%	85.5 [80]	1.7 [99]	-27.5 [85]
▲	Changeup	14.6%	84.9 [98]	-10.7 [103]	-29.6 [93]
✕	Splitter				
▽	Slider	22.6%	84.2 [99]	4.7 [99]	-30.2 [108]
◇	Curveball	11.1%	77.7 [97]	8.9 [104]	-51.7 [92]
⊕	Slow Curveball				
✱	Knuckleball				
▼	Screwball				

Hyun-jin Ryu LHP

Born: 03/25/87   Age: 32   Bats: R   Throws: L
Height: 6'3"   Weight: 250   Origin: International Free Agent, 2013

YEAR	TEAM	LVL	AGE	W	L	SV	G	GS	IP	H	HR	BB/9	K/9	K	GB%	BABIP
2016	OKL	AAA	29	0	1	0	3	3	9²	17	2	0.0	8.4	9	44%	.441
2016	RCU	A+	29	1	1	0	5	5	18	15	2	0.5	7.0	14	45%	.241
2016	LAN	MLB	29	0	1	0	1	1	4²	8	1	3.9	7.7	4	50%	.412
2017	LAN	MLB	30	5	9	1	25	24	126²	128	22	3.2	8.2	116	48%	.299
2018	LAN	MLB	31	7	3	0	15	15	82¹	68	9	1.6	9.7	89	47%	.281
2019	LAN	MLB	32	9	7	0	23	23	131	122	18	2.5	9.1	132	45%	.294

Breakout: 20%   Improve: 46%   Collapse: 28%   Attrition: 13%   MLB: 94%
Comparables: Chris Capuano, Wandy Rodriguez, James Shields

Just to qualify, injuries aren't good. Period. Having said that, when Ryu gruesomely tore his groin muscle right off the bone it reminded us all that some injuries are, in fact, way grosser than others. That said, it paved the way for rookie phenom Walker Buehler to join the rotation, so maybe there was a silver lining (well, at least for everyone other than Ryu himself). When the southpaw returned to the rotation, he dominated, making nine starts down the stretch, posting a 1.88 ERA and punching out a batter per inning. He also took the ball in Game 1 of the NLDS, tossing seven shutout innings and fanning eight Braves in the process. It was an impressive bounce-back season for Ryu, who spun that success into a qualifying offer from the Dodgers to kick off the hot stove.

YEAR	TEAM	LVL	AGE	WHIP	ERA	DRA	WARP	MPH	FB%	WHF	CSP
2016	OKL	AAA	29	1.76	8.38	3.93	0.2				
2016	RCU	A+	29	0.89	2.00	2.94	0.5				
2016	LAN	MLB	29	2.14	11.57	3.27	0.1	92.7	56.5	11.8	45.5
2017	LAN	MLB	30	1.37	3.77	4.18	2.0	92.3	36.8	11.4	41
2018	LAN	MLB	31	1.01	1.97	2.45	2.7	91.9	37	12.6	49.8
2019	LAN	MLB	32	1.21	3.81	4.13	1.4	91.2	36.9	11.8	45.4

Hyun-jin Ryu, continued

Pitch Shape vs LHH

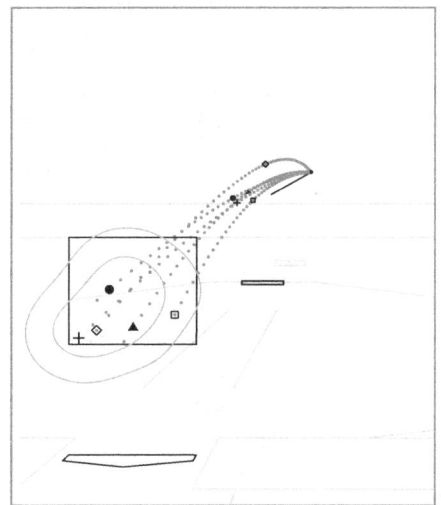

Pitch Shape vs RHH

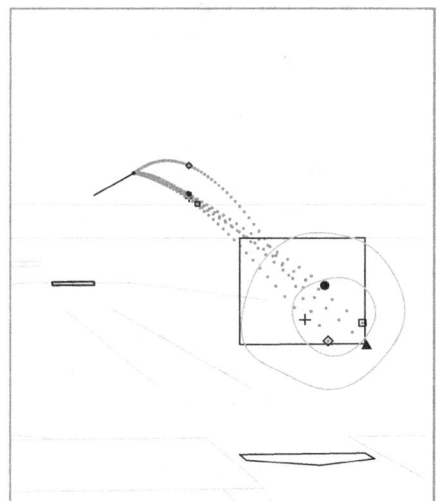

Type	Frequency	Velocity	H Movement	V Movement
● Fastball	31.6%	90.8 [94]	8.5 [92]	-17.4 [95]
☐ Sinker	5.4%	90.2 [89]	13.9 [89]	-21.2 [97]
+ Cutter	24.9%	87.6 [93]	-0.4 [91]	-24.4 [97]
▲ Changeup	18.6%	81.5 [85]	12 [96]	-30.5 [91]
✕ Splitter				
▽ Slider	0.8%	80.2 [81]	-3.3 [93]	-41.7 [74]
◇ Curveball	18.6%	74 [84]	-9.8 [108]	-57.8 [78]
✦ Slow Curveball				
✳ Knuckleball				
▼ Screwball				

Jaime Schultz   RHP
Born: 06/20/91   Age: 28   Bats: R   Throws: R
Height: 5'10"   Weight: 200   Origin: Round 14, 2013 Draft (#428 overall)

YEAR	TEAM	LVL	AGE	W	L	SV	G	GS	IP	H	HR	BB/9	K/9	K	GB%	BABIP
2016	DUR	AAA	25	5	7	0	27	27	130^2	113	12	4.7	11.2	163	43%	.327
2017	DUR	AAA	26	1	0	0	13	0	11^2	10	1	3.1	16.2	21	46%	.391
2018	DUR	AAA	27	2	1	3	32	1	36	44	5	5.8	14.5	58	36%	.464
2018	TBA	MLB	27	2	2	0	22	1	30^1	18	6	5.0	10.4	35	30%	.188
2019	LAN	MLB	28	1	1	0	14	0	15	12	2	4.9	11.8	20	40%	.296

Breakout: 18%   Improve: 32%   Collapse: 9%   Attrition: 21%   MLB: 42%
Comparables: Joel Carreno, Thomas Diamond, Ramon A. Ramirez

After working as a starter though 2016, Schultz covered to a relief role in 2017 and remained there save for one terrible turn as an opener that lasted two-thirds of an inning at the end of the year. He shuttled back and forth between Durham and St. Petersburg, posting big strikeout numbers and high walk totals regardless of the city. Schultz made the brave choice of being a fastball-only reliever who can't locate a fastball, but in his defense he gets enough on it that at least hitters struggle to locate it as well. The result is a live arm and the ability to pitch multiple innings at a time. Yep, that's a Rays pitcher.

YEAR	TEAM	LVL	AGE	WHIP	ERA	DRA	WARP	MPH	FB%	WHF	CSP
2016	DUR	AAA	25	1.39	3.58	3.89	2.2				
2017	DUR	AAA	26	1.20	3.86	1.48	0.5				
2018	DUR	AAA	27	1.86	5.75	3.95	0.5				
2018	TBA	MLB	27	1.15	5.64	4.14	0.3	96.7	80.3	14.4	47.8
2019	LAN	MLB	28	1.35	3.78	4.15	0.1	96.1	80.8	14.5	48.1

Jaime Schultz, continued

Pitch Shape vs LHH

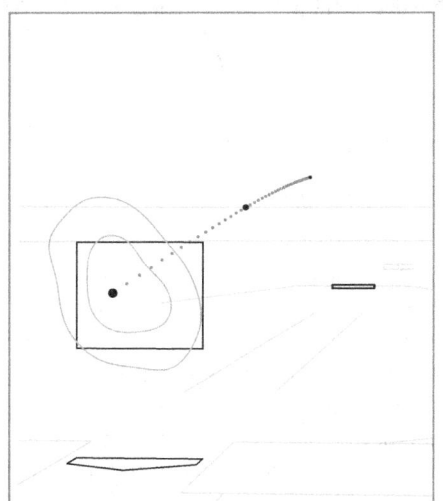

Pitch Shape vs RHH

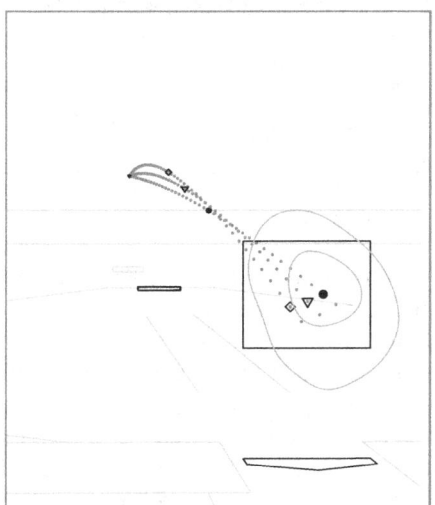

Type	Frequency	Velocity	H Movement	V Movement
● Fastball	80.3%	95.3 [109]	-5.9 [104]	-11.9 [112]
☐ Sinker				
+ Cutter				
▲ Changeup				
✕ Splitter				
▽ Slider	9.8%	86.7 [110]	3.1 [92]	-32 [103]
◇ Curveball	9.9%	81.7 [112]	9.9 [109]	-49.8 [96]
⊕ Slow Curveball				
✴ Knuckleball				
▼ Screwball				

Los Angeles Dodgers 2019

Ross Stripling   RHP
Born: 11/23/89   Age: 29   Bats: R   Throws: R
Height: 6'3"   Weight: 210   Origin: Round 5, 2012 Draft (#176 overall)

YEAR	TEAM	LVL	AGE	W	L	SV	G	GS	IP	H	HR	BB/9	K/9	K	GB%	BABIP
2016	OKL	AAA	26	0	2	0	5	4	16^2	20	2	1.1	9.2	17	38%	.360
2016	LAN	MLB	26	5	9	0	22	14	100	96	10	2.7	6.7	74	52%	.283
2017	LAN	MLB	27	3	5	2	49	2	74^1	69	10	2.3	9.0	74	51%	.294
2018	LAN	MLB	28	8	6	0	33	21	122	123	18	1.6	10.0	136	47%	.322
2019	LAN	MLB	29	10	7	0	40	21	140	134	19	2.6	8.9	138	47%	.298

Breakout: 24%   Improve: 49%   Collapse: 18%   Attrition: 3%   MLB: 91%
Comparables: Taylor Buchholz, Shaun Marcum, Boof Bonser

"I want you to hit me, as hard as you can." It's a notorious line from *Fight Club*, and it's also an instruction given to Stripling from Dodgers pitching coach Rick Honeycutt. Ok, fine, maybe it was more along the lines of "throw your curveball as hard as you can," but still. The result was stark, as the 28-year-old Texan's tunnel on the curve began to mirror that of his fastball, paving the way for more deception and more strikeouts. Stripling cruised to a 1.98 ERA in his first 11 starts, good enough for his first all-star berth. Minor injuries and staff depth limited him to only 10 mediocre starts and some time in the bullpen after July 1, but it was still a breakout campaign for Stripling, who also dabbles as a Series 7 licensed stockbroker. If he maintains this season's production, he'll have a much bigger portfolio to invest and play with in the very near future.

YEAR	TEAM	LVL	AGE	WHIP	ERA	DRA	WARP	MPH	FB%	WHF	CSP
2016	OKL	AAA	26	1.32	3.78	3.02	0.4				
2016	LAN	MLB	26	1.26	3.96	3.28	2.3	93.3	46.5	9.1	45.9
2017	LAN	MLB	27	1.18	3.75	3.23	1.6	94.5	38.4	12	44.1
2018	LAN	MLB	28	1.19	3.02	2.94	3.3	93.8	41.1	12.5	47.3
2019	LAN	MLB	29	1.25	3.80	4.12	1.5	93.2	41.8	11.5	45.9

Ross Stripling, continued

Pitch Shape vs LHH

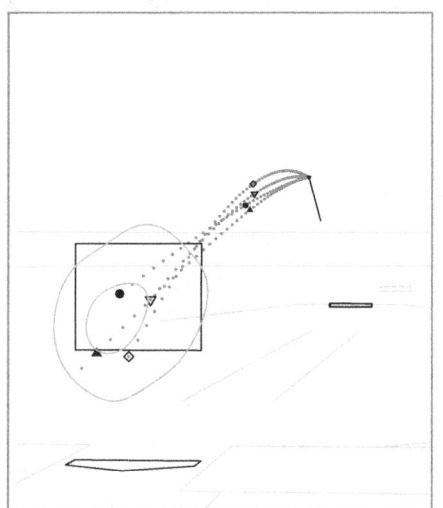

Pitch Shape vs RHH

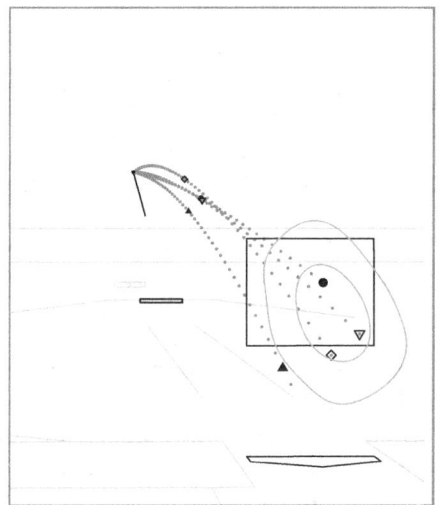

Type	Frequency	Velocity	H Movement	V Movement
● Fastball	41.1%	92.2 [99]	-2.1 [121]	-13.3 [108]
□ Sinker	0.1%	88.3 [79]	-10.3 [119]	-19.8 [102]
+ Cutter				
▲ Changeup	11.0%	84.9 [98]	-9.4 [110]	-26.2 [103]
× Splitter				
▽ Slider	26.2%	87.6 [114]	4.4 [98]	-26.1 [120]
◇ Curveball	21.7%	80.8 [109]	5.2 [89]	-51.1 [93]
⊕ Slow Curveball				
✳ Knuckleball				
▼ Screwball				

Dodgers Player Analysis - 69

Omar Estevez MI

Born: 02/25/98   Age: 21   Bats: R   Throws: R
Height: 5'10"   Weight: 168   Origin: International Free Agent, 2015

YEAR	TEAM	LVL	AGE	PA	R	2B	3B	HR	RBI	BB	K	SB	CS	AVG/OBP/SLG
2016	GRL	A	18	508	46	32	2	9	61	26	121	3	6	.255/.298/.389
2017	RCU	A+	19	502	56	24	3	4	47	33	97	2	2	.256/.309/.348
2018	RCU	A+	20	577	87	43	2	15	84	45	138	3	1	.278/.336/.456
2019	LAN	MLB	21	251	18	10	0	6	25	8	71	0	0	.185/.211/.304

Breakout: 1%   Improve: 4%   Collapse: 0%   Attrition: 2%   MLB: 4%
Comparables: Orlando Calixte, Christian Arroyo, Yamaico Navarro

Blah blah blah development isn't linear blah blah. We've heard it before, and we've said it plenty of times before, but Estevez is the reason the cliche is always apropos. Signed for a cool $6 million bonus in 2015, the Cuban import finally started to put the pieces together during his second stint at High-A, leading the Cal League in doubles and runs, while clocking in at number three with 60 extra-base hits. Sure, hitting in the Cal League helps, but legitimate skill development carried a good bit of the numeric improvement. Estevez refined an already-sweet swing to create better, more consistent line-drive contact. He spent more time at the keystone, likely foreshadowing his eventual position, but he also continued to hold his own at short, a pleasant surprise to pair with his offense-heavy projected profile.

YEAR	TEAM	LVL	AGE	PA	DRC+	VORP	BABIP	BRR	FRAA	WARP
2016	GRL	A	18	508	97	10.6	.322	-2.7	2B(64): 3.0, SS(46): 6.5	1.4
2017	RCU	A+	19	502	71	10.2	.314	1.0	SS(98): 2.7, 2B(22): 0.4	-0.3
2018	RCU	A+	20	577	104	36.1	.344	1.2	SS(74): 2.6, 2B(47): 1.7	1.3
2019	LAN	MLB	21	251	33	-11.8	.231	-0.6	SS 2, 2B 1	-0.9

Jeren Kendall CF

Born: 02/04/96 Age: 23 Bats: L Throws: R
Height: 6'0" Weight: 190 Origin: Round 1, 2017 Draft (#23 overall)

YEAR	TEAM	LVL	AGE	PA	R	2B	3B	HR	RBI	BB	K	SB	CS	AVG/OBP/SLG
2017	GRL	A	21	155	21	5	7	2	18	13	42	5	8	.221/.290/.400
2018	RCU	A+	22	494	68	20	3	12	42	52	158	37	14	.215/.300/.356
2019	*LAN*	*MLB*	*23*	*251*	*24*	*5*	*2*	*6*	*21*	*15*	*91*	*8*	*4*	*.139/.189/.259*

Breakout: 3% Improve: 4% Collapse: 0% Attrition: 4% MLB: 4%
Comparables: Keon Broxton, Adam Engel, Drew Stubbs

Way back in the 90's, there were these things calls Magic Eye books, where readers could see 3D images by strenuously focusing on 2D patterns. For those too young to remember the phenomenon, it was a thing, seriously. Kendall has tools—oh so many tools—and you know what you're *supposed* to be seeing. But thus far those tools haven't started morphing into a clear, discernible picture of a big leaguer. It can be endlessly frustrating. Perhaps Kendall could use a magic eye of his own, as the former Vanderbilt Commodore had the fourth-highest strikeout rate in the Cal League, and is now hitting a meager .216 in 578 plate appearances since he graduated from rookie ball.

YEAR	TEAM	LVL	AGE	PA	DRC+	VORP	BABIP	BRR	FRAA	WARP
2017	GRL	A	21	155	79	2.0	.299	-0.6	CF(24): 3.5, RF(5): -0.4	0.1
2018	RCU	A+	22	494	66	6.6	.305	2.5	CF(92): 1.1, RF(8): 0.8	-1.0
2019	*LAN*	*MLB*	*23*	*251*	*14*	*-15.5*	*.188*	*1.2*	*CF 0, RF 0*	*-1.6*

Gavin Lux SS
Born: 11/23/97 Age: 21 Bats: L Throws: R
Height: 6'2" Weight: 190 Origin: Round 1, 2016 Draft (#20 overall)

YEAR	TEAM	LVL	AGE	PA	R	2B	3B	HR	RBI	BB	K	SB	CS	AVG/OBP/SLG
2016	DOD	RK	18	219	34	10	5	0	18	25	43	1	0	.281/.365/.385
2016	OGD	RK	18	34	7	3	0	0	3	3	8	1	0	.387/.441/.484
2017	GRL	A	19	501	68	14	8	7	39	56	88	27	10	.244/.331/.362
2018	RCU	A+	20	404	64	23	7	11	48	43	68	11	7	.324/.396/.520
2018	TUL	AA	20	120	21	4	1	4	9	14	20	2	2	.324/.408/.495
2019	LAN	MLB	21	251	26	5	2	6	21	15	64	3	2	.184/.232/.303

Breakout: 22%   Improve: 28%   Collapse: 1%   Attrition: 11%   MLB: 29%
Comparables: Francisco Lindor, Daniel Robertson, Jorge Polanco

The lineout for Lux last season indicated that the infielder would need a "strong showing to alleviate creeping doubts about his future." Well, consider those doubts alleviated. The only thing creeping up is Lux's stock as a prospect, with premium bat-to-ball skills, budding pop and a solid eye leading to domination across two levels and what we can only assume is a plaque for being the Dodgers' Minor League Hitter of the Year. A cold-weather product from Wisconsin, land of cheese and *Making a Murderer*, Lux's profile flipped on its head this season, combining his offensive outbreak with only fair defense up the middle. A decent arm and passable athleticism potentially calls his spot at the six into question, but even average defense to pair with a developing bat makes the 21-year-old an awfully interesting prospect.

YEAR	TEAM	LVL	AGE	PA	DRC+	VORP	BABIP	BRR	FRAA	WARP
2016	DOD	RK	18	219	138	16.6	.360	1.1	SS(43): -7.9	0.0
2016	OGD	RK	18	34	159	4.1	.522	0.0	SS(8): -1.3	0.1
2017	GRL	A	19	501	97	19.5	.288	3.4	SS(65): 3.8, 2B(43): 4.0	2.1
2018	RCU	A+	20	404	145	34.3	.374	-1.8	SS(66): -0.6, 2B(17): 0.8	2.2
2018	TUL	AA	20	120	150	11.6	.370	1.3	SS(26): -0.6	0.9
2019	LAN	MLB	21	251	40	-8.2	.220	0.3	SS 0, 2B 0	-0.9

DJ Peters OF

Born: 12/12/95 Age: 23 Bats: R Throws: R
Height: 6'6" Weight: 225 Origin: Round 4, 2016 Draft (#131 overall)

YEAR	TEAM	LVL	AGE	PA	R	2B	3B	HR	RBI	BB	K	SB	CS	AVG/OBP/SLG
2016	OGD	RK	20	302	63	24	3	13	48	35	66	5	3	.351/.437/.615
2017	RCU	A+	21	587	91	29	5	27	82	64	189	3	3	.276/.372/.514
2018	TUL	AA	22	559	79	23	3	29	60	45	192	1	2	.236/.320/.473
2019	LAN	MLB	23	251	26	10	1	11	33	14	98	0	0	.199/.262/.387

Breakout: 9% Improve: 29% Collapse: 5% Attrition: 22% MLB: 52%
Comparables: Greg Halman, Joe Benson, Derek Fisher

If pop artists from the 70s and 80s Frampton and Cetera started an MC duo, you'd likely get DJ Peters, who, as it turns out, is also a strong-armed and athletic outfielder in the Dodgers organization. In the mold of skyscraping sluggers like Aaron Judge and Jayson Werth, Peters does two things prodigiously—sock dingers and strike out. The native Californian achieved one of these two results in nearly 40 percent of his plate appearances, comfortably leading the Texas League this season in both categories. He has thus far defied the expectations for a man his size by holding his own in center, but a likely eventual move to right puts that much more pressure on his prodigious power to play more consistently.

YEAR	TEAM	LVL	AGE	PA	DRC+	VORP	BABIP	BRR	FRAA	WARP
2016	OGD	RK	20	302	200	46.4	.432	0.5	CF(31): 4.5, RF(28): -3.6	2.7
2017	RCU	A+	21	587	118	43.2	.385	0.9	CF(80): -3.5, LF(18): -1.0	0.7
2018	TUL	AA	22	559	95	20.6	.316	-3.6	CF(96): -3.1, RF(29): 1.4	-0.4
2019	LAN	MLB	23	251	76	1.3	.291	-0.4	CF -1, RF 0	0.0

Carlos Rincon RF
Born: 10/14/97 Age: 21 Bats: R Throws: R
Height: 6'3" Weight: 190 Origin: International Free Agent, 2015

YEAR	TEAM	LVL	AGE	PA	R	2B	3B	HR	RBI	BB	K	SB	CS	AVG/OBP/SLG
2016	DDO	RK	18	96	19	5	2	6	26	15	23	8	2	.364/.458/.714
2016	DOD	RK	18	105	13	6	3	7	23	2	30	0	2	.301/.314/.621
2017	GRL	A	19	370	41	13	1	18	48	32	143	6	1	.198/.270/.404
2017	OGD	RK	19	52	8	4	0	3	13	1	16	0	0	.275/.288/.529
2018	GRL	A	20	338	28	13	2	7	33	41	91	5	1	.226/.331/.358
2018	RCU	A+	20	131	36	9	0	15	35	16	31	0	1	.327/.427/.818
2019	LAN	MLB	21	251	21	6	0	11	29	10	98	0	0	.142/.176/.302

Breakout: 6% Improve: 10% Collapse: 3% Attrition: 7% MLB: 14%
Comparables: Domingo Santana, Lewis Brinson, Caleb Gindl

Eyes are bleary and bloodshot. Handwritten scouting reports are strewn in every corner of the office; can recite them by heart. Raw power. High ceiling. Strong lower half. Forceful swing. Limited hit tool? The phrases flash like the neon casino lights, lighting up the Nevada desert like a Christmas tree. Another pull from the whiskey bottle as the old grandfather clock strikes something o'clock in the wee hours of the morning. Unspectacular stat lines littered Rincon's profile since his first rendezvous through rookie ball, making his progress and domination of High-A all the more intriguing and confounding. He walked more. He struck out less. He launched 15 homers in 29 games. It...it looked like progress. It looked like excitement. Just then, a silhouette crept into the doorway. He entered, the ghost of C.J. Retherford morphed with the ghost of Angelo Songco, two Dodger High-A legends. He spoke. "Forget it, Jake. It's Rancho."

YEAR	TEAM	LVL	AGE	PA	DRC+	VORP	BABIP	BRR	FRAA	WARP
2016	DDO	RK	18	96	189	17.0	.431	1.0	RF(15): 1.7, CF(5): -0.2	1.1
2016	DOD	RK	18	105	124	8.5	.364	-1.0	RF(23): 2.0	0.1
2017	GRL	A	19	370	84	5.5	.274	1.1	RF(50): -7.6, LF(15): 2.2	-1.0
2017	OGD	RK	19	52	75	2.9	.344	0.4	RF(2): -0.2, LF(1): 0.1	-0.1
2018	GRL	A	20	338	94	5.7	.301	0.6	RF(48): -0.9, LF(6): -0.7	-0.3
2018	RCU	A+	20	131	175	22.8	.323	1.7	RF(10): 0.5, LF(8): -0.5	1.1
2019	LAN	MLB	21	251	22	-17.5	.176	-0.5	RF -1, LF 0	-2.0

Keibert Ruiz C

Born: 07/20/98 Age: 20 Bats: B Throws: R
Height: 6'0" Weight: 200 Origin: International Free Agent, 2015

YEAR	TEAM	LVL	AGE	PA	R	2B	3B	HR	RBI	BB	K	SB	CS	AVG/OBP/SLG
2016	DOD	RK	17	39	5	4	1	0	15	3	4	0	0	.485/.513/.667
2016	OGD	RK	17	206	28	18	2	2	33	12	23	0	0	.354/.393/.503
2017	GRL	A	18	251	34	16	1	2	24	18	30	0	0	.317/.372/.423
2017	RCU	A+	18	160	24	7	1	6	27	7	23	0	0	.315/.344/.497
2018	TUL	AA	19	415	44	14	0	12	47	26	33	0	1	.268/.328/.401
2019	LAN	MLB	20	251	22	9	0	7	28	6	45	0	0	.218/.247/.347

Breakout: 14%   Improve: 18%   Collapse: 0%   Attrition: 6%   MLB: 18%
Comparables: Carson Kelly, Jake Bauers, Freddie Freeman

A quick Google search for "contact" brings up pages and pages of results for a 1997 Jodie Foster and Matthew McConaughey flick that was, let's say decent if unspectacular. "Extreme contact" brings about plenty of Amazon reviews for tires. While both outcomes are certainly warranted, it's hard to not quibble with Ruiz's exclusion on either search. Sure, you might hope for a few more walks, but whip-quick wrists paired with an uncanny knack for, well, you know, and the Venezuelan wunderkind whiffed a staggeringly infrequent eight percent of the time. That's a hilariously low number for anyone in this baseball universe, and it's truly incredible for a 19-year-old switch-hitting catcher in Double-A. As if that wasn't enough, Ruiz even managed to pop a few more dingers this season to boot, avoiding the "empty average" moniker that usually accompanies high-contact hitters. While he didn't turn up in an extremely specific and limited search, the next option to try might be "super exciting catching prospects that could be really good for a long time." Ruiz would be all over that one.

YEAR	TEAM	P. COUNT	FRM RUNS	BLK RUNS	THRW RUNS	TOT RUNS
2018	TUL	11928	5.3	-0.6	-0.4	3.9
2019	LAN	8818	-1.8	0.0	0.0	-1.8

YEAR	TEAM	LVL	AGE	PA	DRC+	VORP	BABIP	BRR	FRAA	WARP
2016	DOD	RK	17	39	231	7.4	.516	-0.8	C(7): -0.1	0.3
2016	OGD	RK	17	206	140	17.0	.389	-1.6	C(35): -1.2	0.7
2017	GRL	A	18	251	127	15.7	.355	-3.2	C(49): -0.9	0.9
2017	RCU	A+	18	160	129	13.2	.333	0.0	C(37): -0.3	0.8
2018	TUL	AA	19	415	92	8.3	.266	-3.8	C(86): 3.5	0.5
2019	LAN	MLB	20	251	56	-2.6	.240	-0.5	C -2	-0.5

Los Angeles Dodgers 2019

Will Smith   C
Born: 03/28/95   Age: 24   Bats: R   Throws: R
Height: 6'0"   Weight: 192   Origin: Round 1, 2016 Draft (#32 overall)

YEAR	TEAM	LVL	AGE	PA	R	2B	3B	HR	RBI	BB	K	SB	CS	AVG/OBP/SLG
2016	OGD	RK	21	33	4	0	0	1	5	4	1	0	0	.321/.394/.429
2016	GRL	A	21	97	12	1	0	1	7	11	18	2	1	.256/.371/.305
2016	RCU	A+	21	115	13	4	0	2	12	14	31	1	0	.216/.330/.320
2017	RCU	A+	22	305	38	15	3	11	43	37	71	6	2	.232/.355/.448
2018	TUL	AA	23	307	48	14	0	19	53	36	75	4	0	.264/.358/.532
2018	OKL	AAA	23	98	9	4	0	1	6	7	37	1	0	.138/.206/.218
2019	LAN	MLB	24	64	7	2	0	3	8	5	22	0	0	.190/.254/.379

Breakout: 9%   Improve: 15%   Collapse: 0%   Attrition: 15%   MLB: 30%
Comparables: Andrew Knapp, Michael McKenry, Josh Donaldson

Now this is a story all about how this dude became one of the best framers around. And I'd like to take a minute, 'cause it ain't no myth, I'll tell you a little tale about a guy named Will Smith. Ahem. A beanball-induced

YEAR	TEAM	P. COUNT	FRM RUNS	BLK RUNS	THRW RUNS	TOT RUNS
2018	OKL	2087	1.2	0.0	0.0	2.1
2018	TUL	4187	7.0	0.1	0.6	8.4
2019	LAN	2341	1.4	-0.1	0.1	1.4

broken hand cut short Smith's first foray into Double-A, but the former Louisville Cardinal picked his breakout right up where he left off, blending strong discipline with above-average contact skills, folding in a burst of pop for the first time in his young career. The backstop struggled with his first taste of the PCL, but the ugly abbreviated stint can likely be written off as a late-season small sample that shouldn't be used to damper this fresh prince's ultimate upside.

YEAR	TEAM	LVL	AGE	PA	DRC+	VORP	BABIP	BRR	FRAA	WARP
2016	OGD	RK	21	33	166	3.2	.296	0.4	C(5): -0.1, 2B(1): 0.0	0.3
2016	GRL	A	21	97	113	6.3	.317	2.0	C(18): 0.0, 2B(3): -0.2	0.6
2016	RCU	A+	21	115	74	1.8	.292	-1.3	C(16): 0.4, 3B(6): 0.9	-0.1
2017	RCU	A+	22	305	102	16.8	.273	-2.0	C(55): 2.7, 3B(6): -1.0	0.5
2018	TUL	AA	23	307	131	25.5	.295	-1.8	3B(33): -1.3, C(33): 7.4	2.0
2018	OKL	AAA	23	98	7	-3.8	.216	1.4	C(16): 1.4, 3B(10): 0.3	-0.4
2019	LAN	MLB	24	64	55	-0.6	.253	-0.1	C 1	0.0

Alex Verdugo OF
Born: 05/15/96   Age: 23   Bats: L   Throws: L
Height: 6'0"   Weight: 205   Origin: Round 2, 2014 Draft (#62 overall)

YEAR	TEAM	LVL	AGE	PA	R	2B	3B	HR	RBI	BB	K	SB	CS	AVG/OBP/SLG
2016	TUL	AA	20	529	58	23	1	13	63	44	67	2	6	.273/.336/.407
2017	OKL	AAA	21	495	67	27	4	6	62	52	50	9	3	.314/.389/.436
2017	LAN	MLB	21	25	1	0	0	1	1	2	4	0	1	.174/.240/.304
2018	OKL	AAA	22	379	44	19	0	10	44	34	47	8	2	.329/.391/.472
2018	LAN	MLB	22	86	11	6	0	1	4	8	14	0	0	.260/.329/.377
2019	LAN	MLB	23	389	44	16	1	11	42	29	62	3	1	.254/.314/.398

Breakout: 14%   Improve: 50%   Collapse: 0%   Attrition: 19%   MLB: 60%
Comparables: L.J. Hoes, Michael Brantley, Desmond Jennings

Per Wikipedia, vertigo can be described as a symptom where a person feels as if they or the objects around them are moving when they are not. Slow yourself down a bit phonetically, and you get Verdugo, an American baseball person that seems stagnant, at least in conjunction with his fellow prospects. It may feel like the Arizonan has been a blue chipper in the system forever, stuck in the minors as his colleagues whiz past him with promotions. However, Verdugo may have logged 874 plate appearances in Triple-A over the better part of two years—mashing to the tune of .321/.389/.452, by the way—but the 22-year-old has consistently been young for his level and still has plenty of time to capitalize on more than just a September call up. His superior contact skills and great eye at the plate should translate nicely to today's homerific game as well—provided that he improves on his ground-ball tendencies—and Verdugo's athleticism, combined with a plus arm, should offer plenty of flexibility in the outfield.

YEAR	TEAM	LVL	AGE	PA	DRC+	VORP	BABIP	BRR	FRAA	WARP
2016	TUL	AA	20	529	119	20.8	.292	-1.2	CF(91): -1.0, RF(30): -0.1	1.2
2017	OKL	AAA	21	495	114	32.4	.340	3.1	CF(59): -5.5, RF(46): 3.1	1.7
2017	LAN	MLB	21	25	86	-1.2	.167	-0.1	CF(6): -0.7, RF(3): 0.0	0.0
2018	OKL	AAA	22	379	130	24.0	.359	-0.5	CF(45): 2.0, RF(31): 2.4	2.2
2018	LAN	MLB	22	86	85	3.2	.306	1.5	RF(16): -0.1, LF(12): 0.2	0.1
2019	LAN	MLB	23	389	90	6.5	.277	-0.6	LF 1, RF 1	0.7

Yadier Alvarez RHP

Born: 03/07/96   Age: 23   Bats: R   Throws: R
Height: 6'3"   Weight: 175   Origin: International Free Agent, 2015

YEAR	TEAM	LVL	AGE	W	L	SV	G	GS	IP	H	HR	BB/9	K/9	K	GB%	BABIP
2016	DOD	RK	20	1	1	0	5	5	20	9	0	4.5	11.7	26	64%	.200
2016	GRL	A	20	3	2	0	9	9	39¹	31	1	2.5	12.6	55	50%	.326
2017	RCU	A+	21	2	4	1	14	11	59¹	61	3	3.8	9.3	61	51%	.335
2017	TUL	AA	21	2	2	0	7	7	33	29	1	6.8	9.8	36	56%	.318
2018	DOD	RK	22	0	0	0	2	2	7	5	0	1.3	12.9	10	71%	.357
2018	TUL	AA	22	1	2	1	17	8	48¹	37	2	8.0	9.7	52	54%	.285
2019	LAN	MLB	23	3	3	0	19	11	55¹	46	6	5.6	9.9	61	48%	.301

Breakout: 8%   Improve: 19%   Collapse: 4%   Attrition: 20%   MLB: 29%
Comparables: Dan Cortes, Jose Cisnero, Zach Phillips

So much has to go right for a blue-chip starting pitching prospect to reach his ceiling. Throwing hard is, well, hard. Developing pinpoint accuracy is harder, and then you have to deal with the possibility that every pitch brings with it the risk of a UCL explosion. It's sort of a marvel that any pitcher becomes good, ever. With Alvarez, all the physical tools are there. His electric fastball hits triple digits with ease, and his wipeout slider is still capable of inducing plenty of whiffs when it's biting. However, his horrific walk totals somehow got worse this year, and the former $16-million-man missed a good chunk of the season with a groin strain and made the majority of his appearances out of the bullpen upon his return. On top of that, Alvarez reportedly went AWOL before a scheduled start in September, which is um, never what you want. The talent is still there with Alvarez, but the days of him having unlimited potential as a starter are in their twilight.

YEAR	TEAM	LVL	AGE	WHIP	ERA	DRA	WARP	MPH	FB%	WHF	CSP
2016	DOD	RK	20	0.95	1.80	2.11	0.8				
2016	GRL	A	20	1.07	2.29	2.49	1.2				
2017	RCU	A+	21	1.45	5.31	3.97	0.8				
2017	TUL	AA	21	1.64	3.55	4.42	0.3				
2018	DOD	RK	22	0.86	1.29	2.01	0.3				
2018	TUL	AA	22	1.66	4.66	4.53	0.4				
2019	LAN	MLB	23	1.45	4.26	4.79	0.3				

Dustin May RHP

Born: 09/06/97 Age: 21 Bats: R Throws: R
Height: 6'6" Weight: 180 Origin: Round 3, 2016 Draft (#101 overall)

YEAR	TEAM	LVL	AGE	W	L	SV	G	GS	IP	H	HR	BB/9	K/9	K	GB%	BABIP
2016	DOD	RK	18	0	1	1	10	6	30¹	37	0	1.2	10.1	34	57%	.394
2017	GRL	A	19	9	6	0	23	23	123	121	8	1.9	8.3	113	52%	.306
2017	RCU	A+	19	0	0	0	2	1	11	6	0	0.8	12.3	15	60%	.240
2018	RCU	A+	20	7	3	0	17	17	98¹	91	9	1.6	8.6	94	58%	.294
2018	TUL	AA	20	2	2	0	6	6	34¹	27	0	3.1	7.3	28	54%	.267
2019	LAN	MLB	21	7	7	0	22	22	115¹	108	15	2.8	7.9	101	50%	.294

Breakout: 4% Improve: 10% Collapse: 4% Attrition: 12% MLB: 16%
Comparables: Brad Keller, Antonio Senzatela, Jhoulys Chacin

Lovingly bestowed the nickname "Gingergaard" on account of flowing locks that burn with the fire of 10,000 suns, May seeks to prove the theory that everything is better with a little ginger. He added a bit of butane to his heater this season, leaving a trail of broken bats and broken spirits in his wake, and he did so in the hitter's haven that is the PCL. Unlike his fellow pole-shaped peers, May has been adept at limiting walks, and while his crossfire delivery might be better served for 80's board games, the combination of deception, stuff and at least two plus pitches make the tall Texan one of the more exciting hurlers in the system.

YEAR	TEAM	LVL	AGE	WHIP	ERA	DRA	WARP	MPH	FB%	WHF	CSP
2016	DOD	RK	18	1.35	3.86	4.29	0.4				
2017	GRL	A	19	1.20	3.88	4.81	0.7				
2017	RCU	A+	19	0.64	0.82	3.57	0.2				
2018	RCU	A+	20	1.10	3.29	4.47	1.0				
2018	TUL	AA	20	1.14	3.67	4.38	0.4				
2019	LAN	MLB	21	1.24	4.22	4.71	0.8				

Dennis Santana RHP

Born: 04/12/96 Age: 23 Bats: R Throws: R
Height: 6'2" Weight: 160 Origin: International Free Agent, 2013

YEAR	TEAM	LVL	AGE	W	L	SV	G	GS	IP	H	HR	BB/9	K/9	K	GB%	BABIP
2016	GRL	A	20	5	9	0	25	14	111^1	84	2	4.5	10.0	124	56%	.290
2017	RCU	A+	21	5	6	0	17	14	85^2	87	5	2.3	9.7	92	50%	.340
2017	TUL	AA	21	3	1	0	7	7	32^2	32	2	6.3	10.2	37	52%	.337
2018	TUL	AA	22	0	2	0	8	8	38^2	26	3	3.3	11.9	51	56%	.258
2018	OKL	AAA	22	1	1	0	2	2	11	10	0	1.6	11.5	14	45%	.345
2018	LAN	MLB	22	1	0	0	1	0	3^2	6	0	2.5	9.8	4	31%	.462
2019	*LAN*	*MLB*	*23*	*2*	*1*	*0*	*5*	*5*	*25*	*22*	*3*	*3.8*	*10.1*	*28*	*48%*	*.295*

Breakout: 10%   Improve: 13%   Collapse: 9%   Attrition: 21%   MLB: 27%
Comparables: Chris Reed, Max Scherzer, Garrett Richards

Like an ACME rocket, Santana enjoyed a meteoric rise in the Dodger organization, exchanging his position at the six for a spot on the mound. After dominating Double- and Triple-A, the 22-year-old got the call to make his big-league debut. Like ACME's most famous customer, however, bad luck consumed the remainder of his campaign. His aforementioned debut came in Coors Field, where he clearly angered the BABIP gods en route to an ERA nearing a baker's dozen. A week later, Santana was scratched from his scheduled start with a balky shoulder. The next day he went on the DL, and the day after he was shifted to the 60-day DL. All that was missing was a handheld wooden sign with the word "Help" crudely written on its face. While a September return to the hill was certainly a welcome sight, it would still be wise for Santana to steer clear of Cal State-Bakersfield, home of the Roadrunners, during the offseason.

YEAR	TEAM	LVL	AGE	WHIP	ERA	DRA	WARP	MPH	FB%	WHF	CSP
2016	GRL	A	20	1.26	3.07	3.56	1.8				
2017	RCU	A+	21	1.27	3.57	3.54	1.7				
2017	TUL	AA	21	1.68	5.51	3.48	0.7				
2018	TUL	AA	22	1.03	2.56	2.72	1.2				
2018	OKL	AAA	22	1.09	2.45	2.58	0.4				
2018	LAN	MLB	22	1.91	12.27	3.78	0.0	95.6	54.3	14.3	44.3
2019	*LAN*	*MLB*	*23*	*1.29*	*3.72*	*4.05*	*0.3*	*95.5*	*56.2*	*14.8*	*45.9*

Julio Urias LHP

Born: 08/12/96 Age: 22 Bats: L Throws: L
Height: 6'0" Weight: 215 Origin: International Free Agent, 2012

YEAR	TEAM	LVL	AGE	W	L	SV	G	GS	IP	H	HR	BB/9	K/9	K	GB%	BABIP
2016	OKL	AAA	19	5	1	0	11	7	45	31	2	1.6	9.8	49	54%	.269
2016	LAN	MLB	19	5	2	0	18	15	77	81	5	3.6	9.8	84	45%	.358
2017	LAN	MLB	20	0	2	0	5	5	23^1	23	1	5.4	4.2	11	43%	.293
2017	OKL	AAA	20	3	0	0	6	6	31^1	20	1	4.3	9.2	32	47%	.253
2018	LAN	MLB	21	0	0	0	3	0	4	1	0	0.0	15.8	7	50%	.167
2019	LAN	MLB	22	6	4	0	32	13	85^1	71	6	3.9	10.2	97	44%	.298

Breakout: 24% Improve: 45% Collapse: 11% Attrition: 16% MLB: 74%
Comparables: Lance McCullers, Brett Cecil, Madison Bumgarner

Everybody loves a comeback story. Everybody loves a heralded young phenom getting the chance to fulfill their potential. Affectionately dubbed "The Teenager," Urias has made fawning parents of us all, swelling with pride during his debut as a 19-year-old prodigy, and rooting unconditionally for a safe and healthy return to the bump after shoulder surgery limited him to 70 1/3 innings over the last two seasons. Well, the southpaw is back. No longer a teenager worrying about borrowing the car keys and going to the homecoming dance (those are still teenager things, right?), Urias can now shift his attention to full-on adult things like maintaining his fastball velocity and taking the ball every fifth day for the crown jewel of the country's second biggest media market. In his brief return to the big club, Urias ran his heater up to 97 mph, and showed enough in a small sample to surprise on both the NLCS and World Series rosters. Better yet, Dave Roberts declared that Urias would be built back up as a starter for 2019. So far, so good. And yet, we still worry.

YEAR	TEAM	LVL	AGE	WHIP	ERA	DRA	WARP	MPH	FB%	WHF	CSP
2016	OKL	AAA	19	0.87	1.40	2.66	1.4				
2016	LAN	MLB	19	1.45	3.39	3.42	1.7	95.4	55.8	11.7	44.3
2017	LAN	MLB	20	1.59	5.40	5.35	0.1	95.2	52	10.2	43.2
2017	OKL	AAA	20	1.12	2.59	2.97	0.9				
2018	LAN	MLB	21	0.25	0.00	1.89	0.1	95.4	69	22.4	58.6
2019	LAN	MLB	22	1.28	3.14	3.49	1.5	95.3	57.7	12.3	52

Los Angeles Dodgers 2019

Mitch White RHP
Born: 12/28/94 Age: 24 Bats: R Throws: R
Height: 6'4" Weight: 207 Origin: Round 2, 2016 Draft (#65 overall)

YEAR	TEAM	LVL	AGE	W	L	SV	G	GS	IP	H	HR	BB/9	K/9	K	GB%	BABIP
2016	GRL	A	21	0	0	0	8	4	16	3	0	3.4	11.2	20	72%	.094
2017	RCU	A+	22	2	1	0	9	9	38^2	26	0	3.7	11.4	49	64%	.286
2017	TUL	AA	22	1	1	0	7	7	28	17	2	4.2	10.0	31	51%	.217
2018	TUL	AA	23	6	7	0	22	22	105^1	114	12	2.9	7.5	88	49%	.317
2019	LAN	MLB	24	6	6	0	21	21	87^2	79	12	3.6	8.4	82	49%	.291

Breakout: 11% Improve: 20% Collapse: 11% Attrition: 25% MLB: 41%
Comparables: Kyle Weiland, Blake Wood, Scott Barlow

Your assessment of White's 2018 might hinge on your outlook in life (you know, not to get too deep or anything). The sunshine and puppy dogs version of the former second rounder's campaign centers around his career high in innings. Meanwhile, on the glass-half-empty side sits basically everything else. White certainly got off on the wrong foot, logging an ERA touching 10.00 through five May starts, and his stat line and velocity both never really recovered. He's not particularly young and it's hard to envision him as anything more than a back-end starter the Dodgers don't have room for. It may be time for the Dodgers to pull the bullpen card and see if his stuff jumps (and his arm stays attached) in shorter bursts.

YEAR	TEAM	LVL	AGE	WHIP	ERA	DRA	WARP	MPH	FB%	WHF	CSP
2016	GRL	A	21	0.56	0.00	3.32	0.3				
2017	RCU	A+	22	1.09	3.72	2.78	1.1				
2017	TUL	AA	22	1.07	2.57	3.08	0.7				
2018	TUL	AA	23	1.41	4.53	5.32	0.0				
2019	LAN	MLB	24	1.30	4.46	4.98	0.3				

LINEOUTS

Hitters

HITTER	POS	TEAM	LVL	AGE	PA	R	2B	3B	HR	RBI	BB	K	SB	CS	AVG/OBP/SLG	DRC+	WARP
Jeter Downs	2B	DYT	A	19	524	63	23	2	13	47	52	103	37	10	.257/.351/.402	122	0.8
Rocky Gale	C	OKL	AAA	30	318	24	14	2	4	34	12	50	1	2	.281/.305/.383	80	1.7
	C	LAN	MLB	30	2	0	0	0	0	0	0	1	0	0	.000/.000/.000	90	0.0
Starling Heredia	OF	GRL	A	19	220	18	9	1	6	26	16	81	3	0	.182/.245/.325	49	-1.7
Paulo Orlando	RF	KCA	MLB	32	93	6	3	0	0	5	3	25	0	0	.167/.194/.200	52	-0.3
	RF	OMA	AAA	32	311	46	17	2	12	41	17	58	2	0	.270/.319/.467	106	0.1
Edwin Rios	3B	OKL	AAA	24	341	45	25	0	10	55	23	110	0	1	.304/.355/.482	116	0.1
Andrew Toles	LF	OKL	AAA	26	275	43	17	1	7	39	13	56	3	2	.306/.345/.461	107	0.6
	LF	LAN	MLB	26	32	5	2	0	0	4	2	8	1	0	.233/.281/.300	81	0.0
Connor Wong	C	RCU	A+	22	431	64	20	2	19	60	38	138	6	2	.269/.350/.480	114	1.2

As a promising defender behind the dish, **Diego Cartaya** signed a $2.5 million contract as a 16-year-old out of Venezuela, immediately making him one of the richest, let's say, 83,500 teenagers in Los Angeles. Reality show pending. ⚾ In his first full pro season **Jeter Downs** flashed his namesake's shortstop range, but not his namesake's blinkered refusal to move to a more appropriate defensive home; now fully ensconced at the keystone, the juice in his bat and a broad set of average tools will likely carry him to The Show. ⚾ Despite a name perhaps more fitting for an SEC defensive backs coach, **Rocky Gale** once again displayed extraordinary framing skills behind the dish. Those skills haven't translated to the batter's box, however, and a career .637 minor-league OPS likely keeps him relegated to third catcher status. ⚾ **Starling Heredia** followed up a breakout 2017 with a pretty middling 2018, a reminder that sometimes electric young superstars with unlimited potential turn into Shia Labeouf, and other times they turn into, well, Shia Labeouf. ⚾ Being second-best at something is usually something to be proud of, but as the second-best Brazilian position player in major-league history, **Paulo Orlando** would prefer that this particular club held more members than him and Yan Gomes. Any chance to eclipse Gomes will have to come with another club, as the Royals have plenty of younger options for "offensively-challenged righty platoon bat" and cut ties with Orlando after the 2018 season. ⚾ As usual, **Edwin Rios** hit a lot this year, but he also hit for less power and started the season on the shelf due to an ominous, undisclosed injury. To boot, if his defense takes another step back, it might fall off the side of the boat. ⚾ A balky hammy and a crowded big-league outfield conspired to keep **Andrew Toles** from showing he can maintain above-average offensive performance more than 120 at-bats at a time. ⚾ The Dodgers saw an Austin Barnes-type when drafting athletic, positionally-flexible backstop **Connor Wong**, which has already made the major-league version very uncomfortable.

Los Angeles Dodgers 2019

Pitchers

PITCHER	TEAM	LVL	AGE	W	L	SV	G	GS	IP	H	HR	BB/9	K/9	K	GB%	WHIP	ERA	DRA	WARP
J.T. Chargois	OKL	AAA	27	1	0	0	11	0	15	13	0	4.2	5.4	9	47%	1.33	1.80	3.74	0.2
	LAN	MLB	27	2	4	0	39	0	32^1	26	4	4.2	11.1	40	63%	1.27	3.34	3.33	0.6
Yimi Garcia	OKL	AAA	27	1	0	1	14	0	14^2	16	2	0.0	8.6	14	42%	1.09	4.30	2.23	0.5
	LAN	MLB	27	1	2	0	25	0	22^1	29	7	1.6	7.7	19	36%	1.48	5.64	6.19	-0.3
Tony Gonsolin	RCU	A+	24	4	2	0	17	17	83^2	72	5	2.8	11.4	106	38%	1.17	2.69	4.03	1.3
	TUL	AA	24	6	0	0	9	9	44^1	32	3	3.2	9.9	49	39%	1.08	2.44	3.45	1.0
Marshall Kasowski	GRL	A	23	0	1	0	15	1	28	13	1	5.8	15.8	49	57%	1.11	2.57	3.27	0.5
	RCU	A+	23	2	0	4	16	0	23^2	10	1	4.2	16.7	44	44%	0.89	1.14	1.80	0.9
	TUL	AA	23	0	0	1	10	0	13	7	2	6.2	12.5	18	31%	1.23	2.77	3.83	0.2
Adam McCreery	MIS	AA	25	2	5	2	34	0	47	48	1	6.3	11.7	61	57%	1.72	3.83	3.43	0.8
	ATL	MLB	25	0	0	0	1	0	1	4	0	0.0	18.0	2	40%	4.00	18.00	8.51	0.0
	GWN	AAA	25	0	0	0	8	0	7^2	3	0	4.7	11.7	10	87%	0.91	2.35	1.73	0.3
Kevin Quackenbush	CIN	MLB	29	0	1	0	10	0	9	13	3	6.0	7.0	7	38%	2.11	11.00	6.39	-0.2
	LOU	AAA	29	1	2	25	47	0	47	39	2	2.1	10.7	56	34%	1.06	2.68	2.97	1.2
Josh Sborz	TUL	AA	24	3	1	6	13	0	16^1	11	1	2.8	13.2	24	35%	0.98	2.76	2.21	0.5
	OKL	AAA	24	1	1	0	33	0	37	38	0	3.6	11.4	47	43%	1.43	4.38	3.64	0.6
Jordan Sheffield	RCU	A+	23	1	3	0	14	7	34	39	8	5.3	10.6	40	44%	1.74	6.88	4.83	0.2
Josh Smoker	PIT	MLB	29	0	0	0	7	0	5^2	11	2	7.9	3.2	2	25%	2.82	11.12	9.90	-0.3
	IND	AAA	29	3	1	0	32	0	35	32	4	3.1	10.0	39	35%	1.26	2.83	3.41	0.7
	DET	MLB	29	0	0	0	1	0	1^2	0	0	10.8	10.8	2	0%	1.20	0.00	4.43	0.0
	TOL	AAA	29	0	1	0	10	0	10^1	13	0	3.5	9.6	11	28%	1.65	5.23	3.22	0.2
Brock Stewart	LAN	MLB	26	0	1	0	9	2	17^2	23	4	4.6	7.1	14	47%	1.81	6.11	5.35	-0.1
	OKL	AAA	26	3	3	0	19	19	96^1	83	7	2.7	7.5	80	41%	1.16	2.99	3.42	2.3

J.T. Chargois flirted with 99 mph and a slider that got grounders almost three-quarters of the time, but his return to the big leagues was spoiled by nerve irritation in his neck that cost the righty over a month of the season. ⓧ Two truths and a lie about **Yimi Garcia**: He pitched for the first time since 2016, his velocity was the highest since 2015 and he served up almost three dingers per nine innings. Oops, that's three truths. ⓧ One of the words to describe **Erik Goeddel's** 2018 season is "whiffy" (I know, but we're making it happen), as the righty tallied one of the better swinging strike rates in all of baseball. Sadly, the other descriptor is "injured" as frequent DL stints led to an August shut down. ⓧ A former two-way player at St. Mary's, **Tony Gonsolin** flew up prospect lists, carving up two levels thanks to a mid-90s fastball, sharp breaking ball and a sick mustache straight out of a 1970s B-movie. ⓧ The Dodgers failed to sign their first-rounder, leaving West Virginia power arm **Michael Grove** as the crown jewel of the draft class. He'll hope to reclaim his mid-90s heater and high-spin-rate slider upon his recovery from Tommy John surgery. ⓧ No hurler in the minor leagues averaged more strikeouts per nine innings than **Marshall Kasowski**, whose unorthodox delivery and significantly improved control helped the former 13th rounder mow through three levels in 2018. ⚾ The Dodgers took a $2 million flyer on **Tom Koehler** in what turned out to be their biggest offseason splurge. Sadly the New York native injured his shoulder in Spring Training and was shut down for good following surgery in July. ⚾ It was the best of times and it was the worst of times for **Adam Liberatore** this season. He closed out a team no-hitter in May, but nagging injuries shut him down for good in August, when he was released. He'll need that second city soon. ⚾ If massive lefties with stuff are your jam, **Adam McCreery**'s spot on the chart is somewhere between no. 1 hit and Pitbull. Control isn't his friend, but he definitely has a major-league arm. ⚾ **Kevin Quackenbush** could provide some bullpen depth, assuming he finds a way to transfer those minor league ratios to the majors again. The Dodgers will soon find out if they should have just stuck with one of their many birds in hand. ⚾ Righty **Josh Sborz** completed his first full season as a reliever, nearly doubling his strikeout rate in just over 50 innings across Double- and Triple-A. ⚾ **Jordan Sheffield** spent his season collecting strikeouts, walks, homers and days spent on the DL with a "mild" forearm strain. Since three of those four are less than ideal, Sheffield is the human version of the gritted teeth emoji. ⚾ Lefty reliever **Josh Smoker** was designated for assignment by two teams and released by a third. He may not want a fourth opinion, but here it is: pretty cool name for a guy with a fastball. ⚾ Hop on the I-40 west for about 1,300 miles before taking the I-5 straight to Dodger Stadium. It's the road from Oklahoma City to Los Angeles that **Brock Stewart** travelled six times in 2018, with middling big-league results along the way.

Dodgers Prospects

The State of the System:
The Dodgers system is coming towards a dip in their org cycle, but still has some very cool high end talent at the top.

The Top Ten:

1. Alex Verdugo OF
OFP: 70   Likely: 60   ETA: Debuted in 2017
Born: 05/15/96   Age: 23   Bats: L   Throws: L   Height: 6'0"   Weight: 205
Origin: Round 2, 2014 Draft (#62 overall)

The Report: There's little to say about Verdugo that hasn't been said a hundred times. He parlays an excellent approach at the plate with double-plus contact ability into a high OBP offensive profile where any power is a bonus. Verdugo's power started to appear more in Triple-A last year and he's ready to see if he can translate that success to the highest level.

Defensively, he doesn't look like he can play center at this point, due to fringy range for the position. Good instincts and a plus arm still should allow him to be an above-average corner outfielder. Overall, Verdugo profiles as a low-risk corner outfielder with upside if he can tap into more of the raw power that he's shown in BPs for years.

The Risks: Very Low. Verdugo is ready to learn and adjust at the MLB level. A high OBP/contact combo make him an extremely low flameout risk and the power is cooking along nicely.

Ben Carsley's Fantasy Take: Verdugo is a fairly boring fantasy prospect, but that doesn't make him an inherently bad one. There's no OF1 ceiling here, but Verdugo could develop into a well-rounded fantasy OF3 in deeper leagues. Perhaps a fantasy OF 4/5 outfielder outcome is more likely, but Verdugo is among the safest bets in the minors to provide value in some capacity. That's good enough to make him a top-50 dude despite the low-ish ceiling.

2. Dustin May RHP
OFP: 70   Likely: 60   ETA: 2020
Born: 09/06/97   Age: 21   Bats: R   Throws: R   Height: 6'6"   Weight: 180
Origin: Round 3, 2016 Draft (#101 overall)

The Report: Dustin May is fun. He is a 6'6" lanky athlete with surprising body control given the length of his frame. He is a good athlete with quick twitch and a fun demeanor on the mound. He generates plus arm speed and good spin rates.

May has a plus fastball that sits in the mid-90's with heavy sink. He also throws a plus breaking ball with good depth and high spin and has advanced feel for the pitch. He'll also show an average mid-80s changeup with good arm speed and average tumble. His feel for the changeup will need to improve, but the three-pitch mix gives May weapons to use deep into a game, and he can always fall back on his plus sinker to generate weak contact.

In addition to the quality repertoire, May has above-average command due to his body control and athleticism. He locates well low in the zone with the sinker and can throw his breaking ball for strikes or break it off the plate at will. Overall, his pitch mix and command should allow him to develop into a No. 3 starter with upside from there if he can improve his command and changeup consistency.

The Risks: Medium. May is a pitcher and that automatically comes with some risk, but he has good pitchability and a quality three-pitch mix. He just needs to improve the consistency of command before he's ready.

Ben Carsley's Fantasy Take: A clear-cut top-101 arm, May will likely fall somewhere in the middle third of the list in the top-half of the glut of good-not-great fantasy arms who'll be ready soonish. The upside here isn't crazy, but May shouldn't hurt you in any one category while contributing solidly across the board. I expect him to develop into a very solid fantasy SP4 who occasionally teases more upside.

3. Keibert Ruiz C   OFP: 70   Likely: 55   ETA: 2020
Born: 07/20/98   Age: 20   Bats: B   Throws: R   Height: 6'0"   Weight: 200
Origin: International Free Agent, 2015

The Report: The switch-hitting Ruiz is one of the most impressive young prospects in the game, thanks to a combination of polish, elite coordination, and quickness. Even better, he's proven adept at making in-season adjustments and improvements.

Ruiz uses his elite bat-to-ball ability to make consistent, quality contact from a compact swing. He's able to adjust his swing to location and understands how to put the ball on a line to all fields. He has above-average raw power, and although the swing doesn't tap fully into it yet, he can put a charge into the ball, especially when he gets out in front. The one downside to his offensive profile is that he can get over-aggressive, which often leads to weak contact.

Ruiz's framing is a work in progress, but improved over the course of the season. He often stabs at balls low in the zone, which can make it hard to get the call. Overall though, he's still an average receiver, due to his soft hands. He has an average arm, but his lightning quick transitions and excellent footwork allow him to effectively control the run game.

Ruiz has significant offensive upside and should be an average defensive catcher. His contact abilities and raw power should make him one of the better catchers in the league, and if he's able to improve his patience at the plate, he could be one of the best offensive backstops in baseball.

The Risks: Medium. Ruiz has shown both a polish and ability to quickly adjust well beyond his years. His ability to handle a pitching staff and excellent coordination give him a high floor at the plate and behind it.

Ben Carsley's Fantasy Take: Ruiz is pretty obviously the second-best dynasty catching prospect in the game (behind Francisco Mejia), and he's a lock to make our dynasty top-101. At the risk of repeating myself, please remember that Ruiz's MLB eta and fantasy impact ETA are likely quite different. That being said, Ruiz has all the tools necessary to develop into a consistent top-7 option at the position. This is a bad position, but he's a good one.

4. Will Smith   C   OFP: 60   Likely: 50   ETA: Late 2019
Born: 03/28/95   Age: 24   Bats: R   Throws: R   Height: 6'0"   Weight: 192
Origin: Round 1, 2016 Draft (#32 overall)

The Report: The Dodgers are flush with potentially impact catchers. Smith is another advanced receiver who has a real shot to become a force at the plate. Smith combines good feel for barrel with an excellent approach that helps his offensive tools play up significantly. The swing can get long, but it allows him to tap into more of his above-average raw power. Smith struggles with quality breaking stuff, but his other tools mitigate that to an extent.

Smith is an above-average receiver with a good understanding of how to handle counts and the pitcher. He has a plus arm and good footwork that will allow him to control the running game effectively. The combination of a solid offensive profile on top of an above-average defensive projection portend a future as a regular behind the plate. There's also room for more if his pitch recognition takes a step forward.

The Risks: Medium. Contact is the one concern with Smith, and it makes him a riskier bet. Other than that, the profile is fairly low risk, as he's a quality defensive catcher with good coordination and polish.

Ben Carsley's Fantasy Take: While I love Ruiz as a dynasty prospect I'm considerably less enthused by Smith. Sure, he's got solid upside as someone with potential catcher eligibility who can hit for power. But I don't fully trust his hit tool, and lots of these tweener positional guys tend to get lost in the shuffle: for every Russell Martin, there are many an Austin Barnes or Blake Swihart, etc. Smith is a top-150 guy due to the upside and proximity, but he won't be on my personal top-101.

5. Gavin Lux SS

OFP: 55   Likely: 50   ETA: 2020
Born: 11/23/97   Age: 21   Bats: L   Throws: R   Height: 6'2"   Weight: 190
Origin: Round 1, 2016 Draft (#20 overall)

The Report: Lux had about as good and complete a season as a prospect can have, both statistically and developmentally. On the latter he performed at a consistently high level throughout his ~four months at Rancho, and then again after a promotion to Double-A. More impressively though, he earned the numbers. His patient approach facilitated in-zone aggressiveness without sacrificing his command of the zone along the way. He added plane and loft gradually to increase pull and lift balls without compromising outer-third coverage. He managed to improve his reactions, lateral agility, and quickness while growing into a larger, rapidly maturing frame.

His raw reads in the field and digs out of the blocks on stolen base attempts could use refinement, but these are minor nits to pick. His above-average speed and demonstrated work ethic suggests potential for improvement on the bases, and despite its limitations, the arm plays up a bit with consistent accuracy and body positioning on his throws. He should be good enough to stay at the six for at least a few years.

The Risks: Low. He's got talent, pedigree, and impressive demonstrated growth all working on his side. This is a significantly higher-probability 21-year-old than most.

Ben Carsley's Fantasy Take: Generally when we talk about "pop-up" prospects, we're referring to guys with big upside who finally saw their tools click. That's not the case with Lux—his upside is fairly low, but his ceiling is quite high as a dude who should be able to play nearly every day for a contending team. Is there some risk that Lux becomes just a super-utility dude in what will be a crowded Dodgers infield? Sure. But if we zoom out, Lux will likely be a starter at second or short for the majority of his career, at which point he'll be an unexciting but very reasonable MI option in deeper leagues. The probability and proximity here are enough to make Lux a top-101 guy, albeit on the back-half of the list.

6. Dennis Santana RHP

OFP: 55   Likely: 50   ETA: Debuted in 2018
Born: 04/12/96   Age: 23   Bats: R   Throws: R   Height: 6'2"   Weight: 160
Origin: International Free Agent, 2013

The Report: Santana's conversion from gangly shortstop to fireballing hurler took another big step forward, culminating in a welcome-to-the-show-kid debut at Coors Field before a shoulder strain cut the festivities short in early June. Prior to the injury, he continued refining a delivery that had improved significantly over the past couple seasons.

Working out of a proper windup, he's still fairly closed-off into his turn down hill. He's a lot straighter down that hill than he used to be, though there's enough cross-fire and sneaky arm speed that he still generates some deception to help the stuff play up. He'll run the gas up to 97 with huge sink and some run, and he's coaxed along his changeup to a point where the pitch tunnels pretty well and holds the heater's line with decent velocity separation. The slider has quickly evolved into a knockout pitch, with hard vertical action and swing-and-miss potential.

Between all of the pitch movement and standard timing stuff that'll crop up in his delivery, the command and control still aren't great, but he has improved it considerably. Between that and honing the third pitch, he's got a better shot at hanging on to a starting role now than it looked like he'd have at this time last year.

The Risks: High. The shoulder injury is a red flag, and while a 180-inning projection's not the prerequisite it once was for a starting pitching prospect, it'd still be helpful to see how he holds up past 120—a number he hasn't yet hit.

Ben Carsley's Fantasy Take: Santana is a reliever through and through for me. The stuff may be exciting, but add in the injury history and he's a player I'm staying away from in all but the very deepest of formats.

7   Tony Gonsolin   RHP   OFP: 50   Likely: 45
ETA: Health permitting 2019
Born: 05/14/94   Age: 25   Bats: R   Throws: R   Height: 6'2"   Weight: 180
Origin: Round 9, 2016 Draft (#281 overall)

The Report: Gonsolin hopped onto the radar when he added a metric ton of in-season velocity out of the 'pen in 2017, and he remains there after keeping most of it upon returning to the rotation in 2018. He cleaned up a significant spine tilt and smoothed out his progressions to a high three-quarter release, leading to a nice bump in utility for his four-pitch arsenal. The delivery is still on the bumpier side, with some exertion that joggles his command and limits its projection. The gas sat mid-90s and touched 98 in the rotation, and while it's a relatively flat pitch with some homerun vulnerability, it holds plane and he works it effectively north and south.

A tight curveball is his best bat-misser. He also punched up a couple more miles an hour on the hook, and it's now a hard spiker with quality depth and above-average utility when he's on top of it. He'll mix in a slider that flashes average as well, though it's less consistent and lacks great bite and finish. A hard trap-door change rounds things out in the mid-80s, and he made strides in better holding his arm speed to sell and locate the pitch more consistently. If he can continue to refine the feel, it plays well enough off his four-seam line that it, too, has potential to grow into an average pitch.

The Risks: High. The fine command profile's sketchy enough that the reliever risk remains significant, though his arsenal is deep and effective enough that he projects to add value out of the 'pen if it comes to that.

Ben Carsley's Fantasy Take: Gonsolin is maybe worth spot-starting if he forces his way into the Dodgers rotation, but that seems pretty unlikely. Even if he does start, his upside is very limited. You can pass.

8 **DJ Peters OF**   OFP: 55   Likely: 45   ETA: 2020
Born: 12/12/95   Age: 23   Bats: R   Throws: R   Height: 6'6"   Weight: 225
Origin: Round 4, 2016 Draft (#131 overall)

The Report: DJ Peters is one of the most physically impressive players on a baseball field. He is tall, high-waisted with a perfect athlete's build. He looks like he could immediately step onto football field as a premier NFL linebacker. He is also a quick-twitch athlete who moves well for his size and shows quality coordination.

The offensive profile is all power. Peters generates extreme swing velocity with a vicious long stroke that generates double-plus raw. He has quality feel for the barrel and he's quick enough to get around on velocity. Unfortunately, Peters struggles to recognize even below-average breaking stuff or offspeed. This—in addition to his longer levers—means that he has low contact rates, which hinders his ability to tap into that raw pop. Despite the K-rates, Peters isn't an overly aggressive swinger on pitches he does recognize and is more than willing to take a walk, which boosts his overall offensive profile.

Defensively, Peters has fair instincts in the outfield and average foot speed, which translates into average range in right field. That along with a plus arm should let allow him to be an above-average fielder in either corner and an occasional fill-in in center field. The extreme offensive profile and the defensive versatility in the outfield fits the mold of a platoon power bat who can provide pop off the bench in favorable matchups.

The Risks: High. He swings and misses quite a bit, even by 2019 standards. The swing is long and he doesn't recognize spin well.

Ben Carsley's Fantasy Take: Sure, Peters has upside, but between his long swing and pitch-recognition issues he's got a slim chance of reaching it. He's a top-200 guy thanks to the power ceiling, but he's definitely not one of my personal favorites.

9 **Mitch White RHP**   OFP: 50   Likely: 45   ETA: 2021
Born: 12/28/94   Age: 24   Bats: R   Throws: R   Height: 6'4"   Weight: 207
Origin: Round 2, 2016 Draft (#65 overall)

The Report: White is coming off of another season where he missed a good chunk of time due to rehab from injury. When he was on the field, he didn't look quite like the guy we've pumped more aggressively in the past.

White sat in the low 90's with a flat fastball. His cutter flashed above average, but was inconsistent. His upper-70s breaking ball flashed above-average with traditional curveball break, but again the quality was inconsistent and hitters often took advantage. White also threw a below average mid-80s change that he showed consistent feel for, though it lacked quality tumble.

Athleticism is the hardest thing to find again after injury and it plays an important part with pitchers. The velocity, arm speed, and body control play vital roles in pitch quality and command. If White can stay healthy and regain some of the athleticism that the injuries have sapped, it's possible that his breaking ball and cutter could tick up. Until then the profile looks much more like a middle reliever mix where his velocity and arm speed could play up in short stints.

The Risks: High. Injuries and inconsistent mechanics have taken a bite out of White's stuff. His final Double-A appearances were kinda ugly, and he never quite looked like the pitcher who evaluators saw earlier in his career.

Ben Carsley's Fantasy Take: White had some prospect helium a year or two ago. If someone in your league hasn't been paying attention and wants to pay for him based on name value, take advantage. Otherwise you can pass.

10. Josiah Gray   RHP

OFP: 50   Likely: 45   ETA: 2021
Born: 12/21/97   Age: 21   Bats: R   Throws: R   Height: 6'1"   Weight: 190
Origin: Round 2, 2018 Draft (#72 overall)

The Report: Gray has the rawness you'd expect from a cold-weather, young-for-his-class college arm who converted from shortstop. The raw arm strength is there. He sat in the low-90s his last year in college, but in the pros Gray found a bit more velocity as a starter in the Appy, if not quite as much as he showed on the Cape in 2017. He gets good sink on the pitch as well, despite his height and a slot a tick below three-quarters. His best secondary is an advanced low-80s slider that shows plus tilt with late tail, while the changeup is going to need significant refinement. Gray is a premium athlete with big arm speed, but there is effort in his mechanics and he throws across his body a bit. Given the slot, present change, and the better velocity he's shown in relief, Gray might be best-suited for the late innings. For now, he needs starter's reps more than a quicker track to the majors.

The Risks: High. Cold-weather arm, significant reliever risk, only a short season track record.

Bret Sayre's Fantasy Take: If you're looking for an arm to gamble on 50 picks into a dynasty draft this offseason, Gray's not a bad name to keep in mind. That said, the better advice might be to not take a pitcher at all.

Los Angeles Dodgers 2019

The Next Five:

11 **Jeren Kendall   OF**
Born: 02/04/96   Age: 23   Bats: L   Throws: R   Height: 6'0"   Weight: 190
Origin: Round 1, 2017 Draft (#23 overall)

You'd have to look real hard and far for a prospect who had a poorer showing in 2018 than Kendall. His obvious physicality and raw tools remain intact, as Kendall boasts twitchy athleticism and excellent speed in space. While he's still developing his instincts in center, he's fairly quick in his reads and his burst catapults him into hot pursuit of balls in any direction. It's an above-average glove up the middle, with plenty of arm to go with it. There's impressive wiry strength on his frame, too; when he squares a ball in BP the raw power'll flirt with plus.

The swing and approach are just… well, they're awful. His setup is unworkable, with low, stiff hands and no rhythm at all into his load. The weight transfer is wildly inconsistent, the swing length is all over the place, and he has no recourse to alter or cut off a swing once initiated. He doesn't see left-handers at all, he shows below-average recognition of breaking stuff below the zone from either hand, and he'll swing through fat in-zone fastballs from righties with the best of 'em. Most problematically, he demonstrated no ability to buy in to, or really even attempt, necessary adjustments at any point during a full season in High-A. This placement is conditional, to the degree that the tools remain quite loud and in line with the 1:1 potential he once held. But he needs to make a whole bunch of progress with the bat pretty quickly to keep pace, and it currently looks less likely than ever that he one day approaches his lofty ceiling.

12 **Jeter Downs   SS**
Born: 07/27/98   Age: 20   Bats: R   Throws: R   Height: 5'11"   Weight: 180
Origin: Round 1, 2017 Draft (#32 overall)

Downs, the Reds' CBA pick from 2017, found his defensive home this season at second base. Stretched at short, his athleticism allowed for a smooth transition to the keystone. Falling down the defensive hierarchy puts more pressure on his bat, which projects to fringe-average. The good news is that Downs' power continues to develop beyond what scouts projected on draft day. He's not a big guy, but he has above-average bat speed and a swing that generates loft. All the tools grade out close to average, which suggests a career as a second-division starter or solid utilityman.

13 **Edwin Rios   IF**
Born: 04/21/94   Age: 25   Bats: L   Throws: R   Height: 6'3"   Weight: 220
Origin: Round 6, 2015 Draft (#192 overall)

Look, it's an ugly profile. You know it, we know it, everyone knows it. Rios is graceful, but in a big-bodied, lumbering kind of way that just doesn't really cut it quickness-wise at his most frequent position to date, third base. He saw some time in left last year, but bottom-of-the-scale speed really limits the utility out there, too. He's smooth and steady-handed at first, and that helps offset some of the range limitations. Still, the glove's not really an asset there either.

At the dish his approach is aggressive in the zone, as he'll consistently offer at early-count strikes. He works with a long, majestic, flowing swing that relies on exceptional timing and hand-eye to work, and that's usually problematic against high-level pitching. There's a "but," though, and that's why he's here. He'll show the right kind of timing and hand-eye on the regular, and he has continued to hit at every stop along the way. He's strong enough to muscle balls to vacant patches of grass, and he's smart enough to go with balls where they're pitched. The power is the light-tower kind. He's carried an above-average offensive profile all the way to the doorstep of the big leagues, as his type is asked to do, and the skills are there for him to take it to the highest level when the opportunity arises.

14 Connor Wong   C
Born: 05/19/96   Age: 23   Bats: R   Throws: R   Height: 6'1"   Weight: 181
Origin: Round 3, 2017 Draft (#100 overall)

The Dodgers draft athletic catchers will multi-position utility as often as they breathe these days, and the club's third-rounder in 2017 fits the mold to a T. He shows decent receiving chops already, with a strong glove hand that'll hold true around the margins of the zone, though he'll lose focus on the endeavor from time to time and muff balls off the webbing. His blocking technique is similarly inconsistent. There's plenty of agility and body control to suggest (potentially rapid) development, however, and he did indeed show better as the season progressed. The story's the same on his catch-and-throw, as he'll need to tighten up his pop in order to keep an average arm playing acceptably. The good news is that he has the physical tools to do all of these things.

At the plate, his right-handed swing is relatively compact, with surprising strength and situational loft. His AB's aren't always pretty, as he'll get coaxed into expanding the zone and swinging non-competitively on his share of pitches. But he also demonstrates an ability to make quick adjustments within at-bats and come right back to barrel something up a pitch or two later. The hit tool's likely to remain on the fringier side, but there's enough pop and baseline athleticism—he's also a solid-average runner with a frame to hold speed—that the sum of the parts can round into a useful player with passable skills behind the dish and additional versatility around the infield dirt. Double-A will test him, and it may take a bit of time for everything to come together, but there's nice raw material here.

15 Jordan Sheffield   RHP
Born: 06/01/95   Age: 24   Bats: R   Throws: R   Height: 5'10"   Weight: 190
Origin: Round 1, 2016 Draft (#36 overall)

Sheffield battled a forearm strain that cost him half the year and jettisoned him to the bullpen upon return, and he never really looked quite right on either end of the layoff, even as the bullpen role appeared to suit him better. A smaller-sized righty, Sheffield's delivery at present lacks the kind of cohesion and simplicity to suit his frame, and the result is a command profile that flutters at best and dips precipitously from there. The bet here is on the raw stuff, and it is among the system's best. He'll sit mid-90s and hump it up to 98, and while the pitch lacks consistent movement, it'll flash ride and finish consistently enough to dream on. He draws out tight, late break on a slider he'll toggle down into a lower velocity band to land in the zone, and it can miss bats when he takes it down below. There's a changeup that projects for occasional utility, too. Similar to his Quakes (and former Vanderbilt) teammate Kendall, there's too much talent to write him off just yet. The shadows are creeping up right quick, though.

Others of note:

Yadier Alvarez, RHP
On raw stuff, Alvarez remains at or near the top of the system. The problem is that he still only possesses raw stuff, and has not yet demonstrated a sustained interest in putting in the work to refine it. Throwing high-90s comes as natural to Alvarez as breathing; the delivery is beautifully efficient and it should be relatively low-maintenance. It's not, though. He consistently runs into subtle timing issues along the way, leading to poor command in the zone and control around it. It's still easy enough to see the on-paper justification for the $12 million the Dodgers paid him a couple years back, but that outlay (and its matching luxury tax penalty) increasingly looks like a sunk cost. The club flirted with bringing him out of the bullpen at points last season, and that seems the likeliest route ahead. If things ever come together, it's a high-leverage ceiling.

Top Talents 25 and Under (born 4/1/93 or later):

1. Corey Seager
2. Walker Buehler
3. Cody Bellinger
4. Alex Verdugo
5. Dustin May
6. Julio Urias
7. Keibert Ruiz

8. Caleb Ferguson
9. Will Smith
10. Gavin Lux

The top three on this list still includes the same names that headlined last year's tour, though a full season of healthy domination by Walker Buehler and some sophomore exposure for Bellinger's bat sparked a mild rejiggering in our long-term valuation. Seager's lost season should not in any way, shape, or form dampen expectations for another monster season ahead as he returns to the fold fully healed.

Buehler emerged as a true heir of the Ace mantle in LA, which is no light claim for a team still featuring the greatest pitcher of his generation. The young fireballer matured considerably in his pitch design and execution through his first full-time run in the rotation, differentiating a cutter and slider to gain pitchability and increase his early-count, off-barrel contact. And he simultaneously added bat-missing utility in the process. Quite the trick.

For his part, Bellinger provided valuable versatility between first base and center. While pitchers were able to adjust and beat him to his blind spots more regularly, his offensive drop-off still yielded a solidly above-average effort amidst a three-win season. He'll still be just 23 for most of 2019, and there's a reasonable case that he should have retained the second spot on this list. Ordinal quibbles aside, this remains one of the best young troikas under any club's control league-wide.

It's been a many-day's journey through the darkest of nights for former (and really still current) wunderkind Julio Urias. Despite just turning 22 last August, he's already worked his way back from a torn anterior capsule, and that he returned to the bump to sit just a tick-plus shy of his pre-injury velocity already is pretty dang incredible. It's a wildcard of an injury in longer terms, insofar as the list of comparables to survive and thrive off this particular surgery is not real long. But if the stuff and panache he showed once activated turns out to be his new normal, the Dodgers will take it in a heartbeat.

Caleb Ferguson's just a damn good young arm. After debuting in his standard starting role in early June he quickly emerged as a trusted option in Dave Roberts' bullpen during the dog days. The role suits his tough fastball and hard hook from the left side, and while big-league hitters rarely had the pleasure, there's enough changeup and utility against right-handers to suggest a higher ceiling still.

It all adds up to a nice annual reminder of just how well-positioned the Dodgers are to sustain their recent run of success into the foreseeable future. And while the minor-league system has thinned some, the top of it offers promise of a further-still extension of cost-controlled core talent well into the next decade.

Part 3: Featured Articles

The Hole in The Shift is Fixing Itself

Russell Carleton

I've been on a bit of a mission against The Shift of late. I'm not out to get The Shift for the usual reasons that people oppose it. The words "the right way to play the game" won't be found on my lips. If a team wants to pursue a strategy that is within the rules and it works, then by all means, they have my blessing (not that they need it). Instead, my concern with The Shift is a worry that it doesn't work, or at least that it has a flaw that needs fixing.

The data show that while The Shift does a decent job of preventing singles on balls in play (what it's supposed to do), it also increases the number of walks that happen in front of it, and the number of additional walks outweighs the number of singles saved. It's a problem because you can't throw a guy out if he gets to walk to first base.

But the "why" was important. It seemed that The Shift was changing the way in which pitchers pitched. We saw that there were fewer fastballs thrown in front of The Shift than we might otherwise expect, and that pitchers tended to stay out of the strike zone a little more. Not by a lot. In fact, it might not even be visible to the naked eye. The percentage of pitches that are out of the zone goes from 51.0 to 53.3 from a standard defense (two right/two left) to a full shift (three on one side). That difference stands up even after we control for the types of hitters that get shifted against. And it's enough to drive up the walk rate to where it cancels out the benefits that teams thought they were getting with The Shift... and then some.

But there was some hope. I found that when individual pitchers stayed closer to the in-zone/out-of-zone mix that they used without The Shift on, they could still get the benefits of The Shift without the walk problems. So, in theory, a team could simply figure out a way to convince its pitchers to not fall prey to the walk trap and The Shift would once again be their friend.

It's reasonable to think that some teams might be more hip to this idea than others. Maybe some figured it out a year before the others. Maybe they were better at getting the message across to their pitchers. Or, maybe no one has figured it out yet.

Warning! Gory Mathematical Details Ahead!

I used data from 2015-2017, made available through MLB's data portal, Baseball Savant. They are kind enough to note when teams are using an infield shift (three fielders on one side of second base), as opposed to a "strategic shift" (someone's playing a bit out of position, but it's not quite that drastic) or a "standard" alignment.

Since we're doing this by team, I can't just look at raw walk rates, because we know that some teams have good pitchers and others have not-so-good pitchers. Some have a mix of both. I used the log-odds ratio method to take into account a batter's general walking proclivities, and a pitcher's as well, and then shoving them into a binary logistic regression. Then, I asked the computer to generate a specific coefficient for each team's pitchers, for when they went into The Shift and how that affected their walk rate.

Using those coefficients, I was able to project what would happen if a league-average pitcher faced a league-average hitter (which we expect would product a league-average walk rate; from 2015-2017, 7.7 percent of plate appearances ended in a walk) and then just switched his hat. Here's the top five and the bottom five:

Top 5 Teams	Projected Shift Walk Rate	Bottom 5 Teams	Projected Shift Walk Rate
Rockies	6.2%	Rangers	11.2%
Pirates	6.7%	Mets	10.4%
Indians	7.2%	Dodgers	10.2%
Astros	7.3%	Cardinals	9.9%
Braves	7.7%	Tigers	9.7%

There are probably people out there right now trying to figure out what the common thread is among the top and bottom teams. I'm sure, because this is Baseball Prospectus, people are already trying to make the case that sabermetric "early adopters" have some sort of edge here. I think that the more interesting piece is that by the time you get to fifth place in The Shift, we're at league average.

As a sanity check, I examined the issue on a pitch-by-pitch level, looking at how often pitchers threw their pitches in the GameDay strike zone, and again using the same basic methodology and getting team-specific coefficients. The names on the list re-arranged themselves, but the idea was the same, and the two lists correlated with an R of .593.

There's a reason that I don't usually do this type of leaderboard post. I don't really know what the Rockies, Pirates, Indians, Astros, and Braves have in common, or what they have that the bottom five don't. I can put a shrug emoji here and say, "Well, it must be something!" but that seems like a cop-out. Instead, I'd like to present another table and suggest that the table above doesn't even really matter anymore.

Year	League Percent Outside K Zone (Full Shift)	League Percent in K Zone (No Shift)	Difference
2015	54.1%	51.1%	3.0%
2016	53.3%	50.9%	2.4%
2017	52.6%	50.9%	1.7%
2018	52.0%	50.7%	1.3%

The hole in The Shift is fixing itself, and it's coming down really fast league wide. In my earlier work on The Shift, I suggested that until teams stopped having such a huge difference between their out-of-zone rate with and without The Shift on, there would just be too many walks for The Shift to make sense. It seems that all 30 of them have been working toward just that. I once estimated that it takes about 10 years for an idea to filter its way through baseball. At this rate, it looks like teams are going to catch up a lot faster than that. And yeah, they're all saber-smart now.

It's likely that whatever magic it was that the Rockies and Pirates had has made its way to Texas and Queens. Or is at least on its way. And if teams are committing to fixing the walk problem, then it's likely that they will continue shifting and shifting a lot.

And eventually it's going to actually make sense for them to do it.

—*Russell Carleton is a former author of Baseball Prospectus and now an analyst for the New York Mets.*

The State of the Quality Start

Rob Mains

One of the seven things you (probably) didn't know about the 2018 season is that quality starts—defined as a start lasting six or more innings with three or fewer earned runs allowed—as a percentage of total starts cratered to an all-time low of 41 percent. I want to look a little more deeply into this, since it's been a while (May of 2016, to be exact) since I've examined quality starts.

The term *quality start* is credited to *Philadelphia Inquirer* sportswriter John Lowe. It's been derided ever since he coined it in December of 1985. Three runs in six innings? That's a 4.50 ERA! In what world is that a measure of quality?

Let's start with that criticism. It's true that 3 x 9 / 6 = 4.5. (You came here for this sort of high-level math, right?) But it's also true that type of start, meeting the bare minimum for earning a quality start, is unusual. Here's the proportion of quality starts in which the pitcher lasted exactly six innings and yielded exactly three earned runs. (I'm going to confine this analysis to the 30-team era, 1998-present. Almost all data retrieved in this article is via the Baseball-Reference Play Index.)

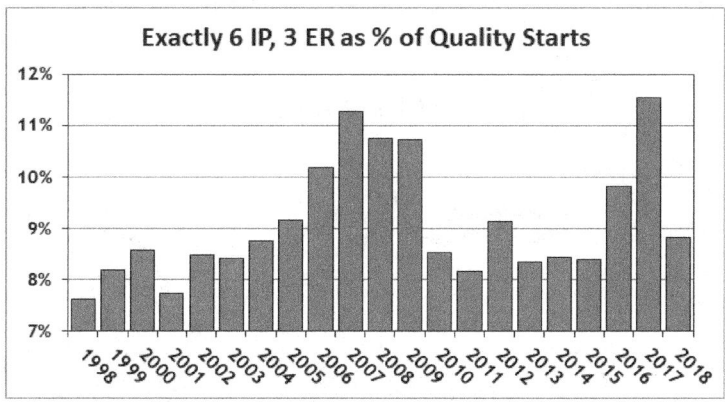

There were 1,997 quality starts in 2018. Only 176, or fewer than one in 11, featured a pitcher going six innings and allowing three earned runs. Put another way, the percentage of quality starts that resulted in a 4.50 ERA (8.8 percent) is less than half the percentage of games in which a batter hit two home runs and his team lost (22.5 percent; 237-69 won-lost). That doesn't impugn hitting two homers.

So if a 4.50 ERA isn't the norm, what is? How good are quality starts?

Pretty good, it turns out. First, on a team level:

Teams receiving a quality start from their pitcher won 68.4 percent of their games in 2018, in line with the 30-team era average of 67.9 percent. A team with a .684 winning percentage wins 111 games. Getting a quality start is definitely a good thing. Individual pitchers throwing quality starts have a higher winning percentage because a big slice of team losses is assigned to a reliever.

If teams do well in quality starts, how well do the starting pitchers do? Again, very well.

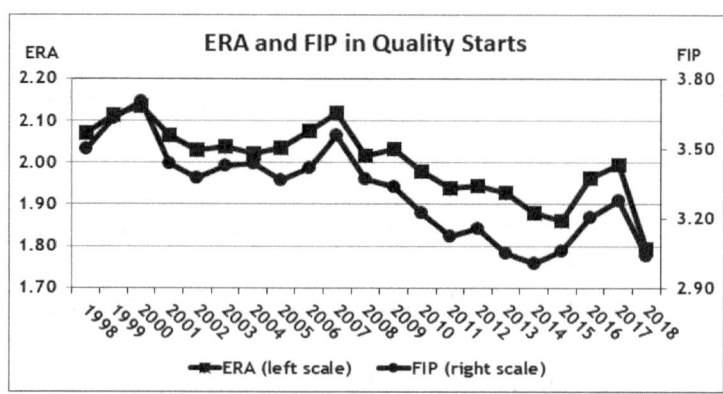

Pitchers in quality starts had a 1.79 ERA (blue line) in 2018, *the lowest in the 30-team era*. Their FIP was higher, 3.04, but still excellent. In the 30-team era, only 2014 had a lower FIP for quality starts, 3.01.

106 - The State of the Quality Start

But, of course, the run environment in 2014 was different. Teams in 2014 scored 4.07 runs per game, the fewest in a non-strike year since 1976. They scored 4.45 runs per game in 2018. So surrendering a 3.04 FIP in 2018 is more impressive than 3.01 in 2014. Accordingly, let's look at ERA and FIP in quality starts relative to league averages.

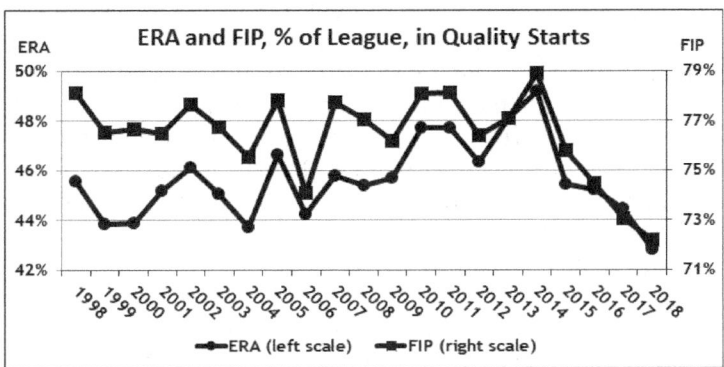

This tells a more dramatic story. Starting pitchers in 2018 gave up a 4.19 ERA and a 4.21 FIP. Starters in quality starts gave up a 1.79 ERA, 43 percent of the league average. Starters in quality starts gave up a 3.04 FIP, 72 percent of the league average. Both of these marks represent lows in the 30-team era.

The takeaway here is this: *Quality starts are better, relative to other starts, than they've ever been over the past 21 years.*

Maybe during the winter I'll look at this over a longer arc of time. For now, though, we can definitively say quality starts are the best they've ever been since the Diamondbacks and Rays joined the majors.

Yet, paradoxically, they're down.

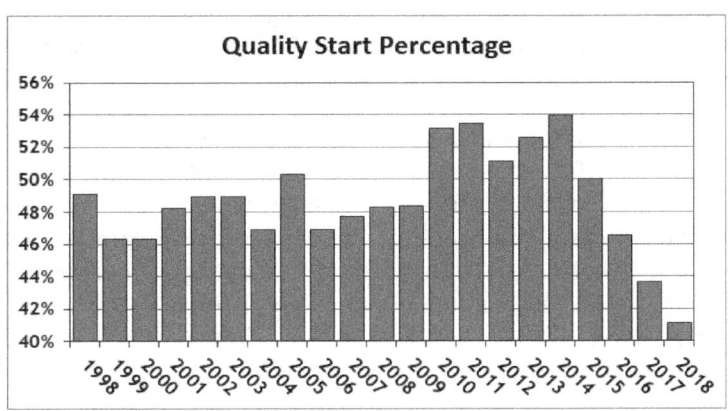

Los Angeles Dodgers 2019

This graph covers only the 30-team era. In my article last week, though, I looked at the years 1908-2018. The result was the same. The 41 percent of starts in 2018 that were quality starts are an all-time low, well below the runners-up: 1930's 43 percent (the year teams scored an all-time record 5.55 runs per game) and last year's 44 percent.

The normal explanation for a dip in quality start percentage is an increase in scoring. When teams score a lot of runs, it's harder for starting pitchers to last six or more innings and limit opponents to three earned runs. From 1998 to 2014, the correlation between runs scored per game and the percentage of starts that were quality starts was -0.94. That means there was an extremely close relationship: More runs, fewer quality starts. Too small a sample? Go back to the start of the Expansion Era, 1961, and the relationship is even more negative, a -0.95 correlation, though 2014.

But that's broken down over the past four years:

- 2015: Runs per game increased from 4.07 to 4.25, quality start percentage decreased from 54.0 to 50.1. Yes, that's a negative relationship, but the regression model would predict a decline of 1.5 percentage points. We got 3.9 instead.
- 2016: Runs per game increased from 4.25 to 4.48, quality start percentage decreased from 50.1 to 46.6. Past experience would suggest a decline of just 1.8 percentage points. We got 3.4.
- 2017: Runs per game increased from 4.48 to 4.65, quality start percentage decreased from 46.6 to 43.6. Again, the direction's right, but the magnitude isn't. Using the relationship from 1998 to 2014, that increase in scoring should've reduced quality starts by 1.3 percentage points, not 2.9.
- 2018: Runs per game declined from 4.65 to 4.45. That should've resulted in the quality start percentage moving in the other direction, rising 1.6 points. It didn't. It fell 2.6 points, as noted, to an all-time low.

Granted, we're talking about just four years here. Maybe they're outliers. But I don't think they are. Quality starts, as noted, are as good or better than ever. But they're rarer than ever as well. And I think I know why.

To get a quality start, you need to allow three or fewer earned and pitch at least six innings. That's 18 outs. Here's a graph showing the number of starting pitchers who limited their opponents to three or fewer earned runs but got pulled after pitching at least five innings but fewer than six:

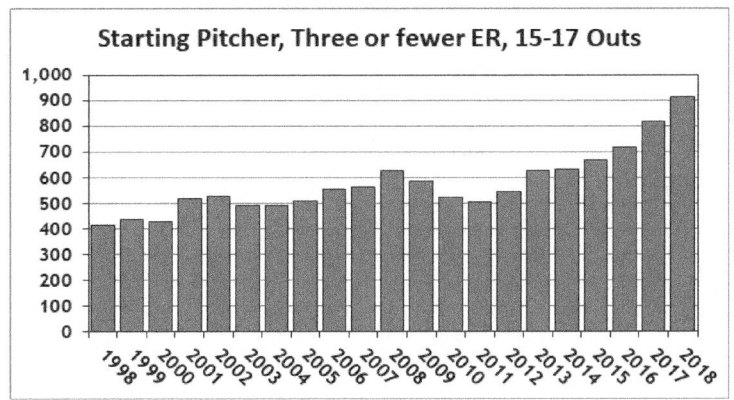

A pitcher getting 15 outs pitched five innings. A pitcher getting 16 outs pitched 5 1/3. A pitcher getting 17 outs pitched 5 2/3. More than ever before, pitchers are being removed from games in which they are within 1-3 outs of a quality start, falling just short of the six-inning finish line. Widespread acknowledgement of the times-through-the-order penalty and a flotilla of available bullpen arms is making the quality start simultaneously both more excellent and more rare.

Which is ironic, given that we saw a new post-war quality start record this season:

Rank	Pitcher	Season	Consecutive QS
1	Jacob deGrom	2018	24
2	Bob Gibson	1968	22
-	Chris Carpenter	2005	22
4	Johan Santana	2004	21
5	Luis Tiant	1968	20
-	Mike Scott	1986	20
-	Jake Arrieta	2015	20
8	Robin Roberts	1952	19
-	Tom Seaver	1973	19
-	Jack Morris	1983	19
-	Greg Maddux	1998	19
-	Josh Johnson	2010	19
-	Jon Lester	2014	19

While there have been longer streaks spread over multiple seasons, no pitcher since World War II threw more consecutive quality starts in one year than Jacob deGrom this year. The fact that he did in a year in which quality starts were the rarest they've ever been adds to the accomplishment.

—*Rob Mains is an author of Baseball Prospectus.*

Heads-Up Hacking—The First Pitch

Matthew Trueblood

Batters fell behind in a higher percentage of all plate appearances in 2018 than in any previous season for which we have pitch-by-pitch data. That kind of granular information goes back only to 1988, but we might safely assume (given all we know about baseball as it had been before that, and as it has been in the years since) that batters have *never* fallen behind at a higher rate than they did last season.

Through the 1990s, the percentage of all plate appearances that began 0-1 hovered in the high 30s and low 40s. In the 2000s, it rose steadily but slowly, through the mid-40s. In 2018, 49.8 percent of all trips to the plate began 0-1. That, as much as anything, captures in microcosm the nature of hitting in MLB today.

A countdown clock toward strike three begins ticking almost the moment a batter takes his place in the box. The league's adjusted OPS+ on the first pitch was higher in 2018 than ever before, and that has been true in most of the last 10 seasons. Batters hit .264/.289/.442 in all plate appearances in which they swung at the first pitch last season, and .241/.330/.395 in all plate appearances in which they took that first offering.

The percentage differences in batting average and isolated power there favor swinging at the first pitch by more than in any season since 1988, while the difference in on-base percentage favors taking by more than ever. If you want to get on base at a decent clip, it's a good idea to be patient, but you run the risk of missing the only chances you'll get to produce power.

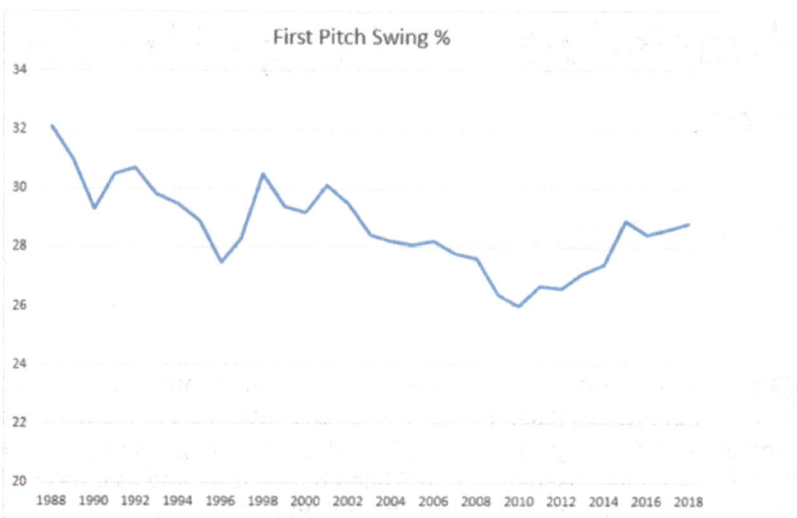

The league swung at the first pitch 28.8 percent of the time in 2018. With the isolated exception of 2015, that's the highest that number has climbed since 2002, but it might not be high enough. With the help of BP research maven Rob McQuown, I looked at the aggregate Called Strike Probability (CSProb) on the first pitch for each season since 2008, when the implementation of PITCHf/x first made measuring that possible. It's risen sharply during that period.

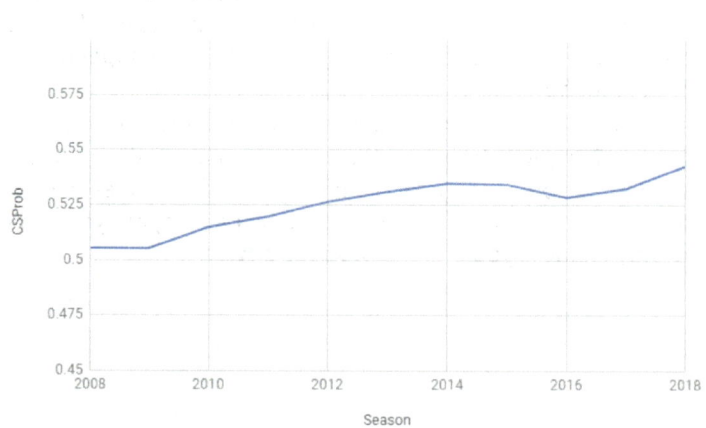

Called Strike Probability, First Pitch of PA (2008-2018)

Called Strike Probability is exactly what it sounds like: a pitch with a given CSProb has roughly that chance of being called a strike, if not swung at. In 2018, a batter who took 100 first pitches from a random sampling of the league's pitchers might expect to fall behind 54 or 55 times—up from 50 or 51 times in 2008. Almost regardless of pitch type (and, notably, especially in the case of fastballs), the first pitch tends to have more of the zone right now than ever before.

Pitchers are better at throwing strikes. They have better stuff, and believe more in their ability to miss bats within the zone. Perhaps most importantly, they know that batters are looking for one thing on the first pitch: a fastball. If they don't get it, they're likely to take the pitch. Check out how the use of sinkers and four-seamers on the first pitch has changed in a decade:

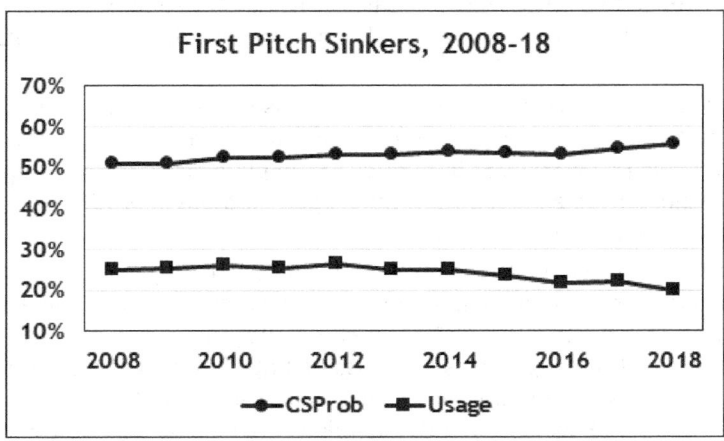

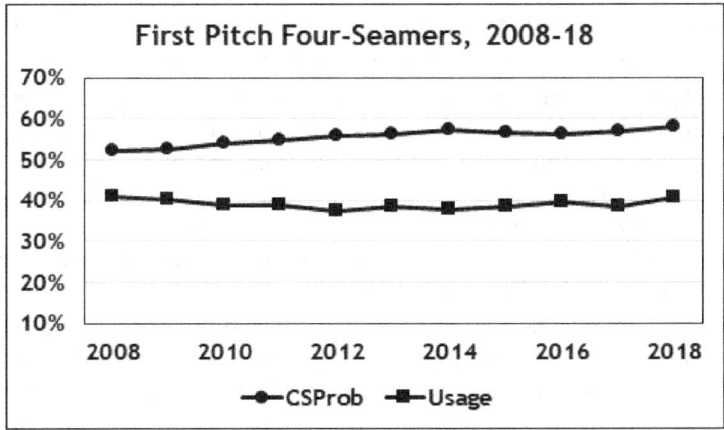

Heads-Up Hacking—The First Pitch - 113

The sinker is losing its place in baseball, but the rate at which pitchers have thrown it on the first pitch hasn't dropped any faster than its usage rate in other counts. Pitchers have actually gone to their four-seamer *more* often to open counts, in the last few years, after a dip in the 2012-2015 period. What's really changed, though, and what shows up in both charts above, is that pitchers are catching more of the zone with first-pitch fastballs than they were a decade ago, or a half-decade ago. They're attacking right away, even with the pitch they know batters are expecting. The message is pretty clear: batters are being too passive.

Sliders, curves, and changeups each have more of the zone when thrown on the first pitch than they did several years ago, too, though the effect is less pronounced. Pitchers have seen the numbers; they know batters are doing better on the first pitch itself. They still feel safe throwing more and better strikes than ever before, figuring they'll come out ahead as long as they keep getting ahead to open each battle.

The Moneyball revolution brought an increased league-wide focus on OBP, which resulted in a de facto mandate to take a more patient tack at the plate. It worked very well for a while, as batters with poor plate discipline were compelled to either adjust or be expelled from the league, and pitchers with poor control were slowly weeded out.

However, concurrent with that revolution, and spurred by it in some ways, was the evolution of the pitching paradigm that now dominates the game. As batters ratcheted up their focus on inflating pitch counts and working walks, pitchers honed theirs on throwing strikes and missing bats. The league's understanding of what makes a good pitcher improved at least as much, from the mid-1990s through the mid-2000s, as its understanding of what makes a good hitter. As amphetamines and other performance-enhancing drugs were phased mostly out of the game, and as PITCHf/x broke onto the scene, individuals and teams learned how to exploit the evolved approaches of even the smartest hitters.

The ability to avoid making outs is still the most valuable one in baseball, but the magnitude of its eclipse of slugging is smaller than ever. To a greater extent than power, on-base skills derive their value from chaining—from the on-base skill levels of the players on either side of a given individual. Eleven years ago, when the housing crisis hit, people learned the hard way that the value of their homes depended a good deal on the values of their neighbors' homes. The same wasn't true, though, of their cars. So it is now, with OBP and SLG.

The global OBP in 2018 was .318. The only seasons since the Dead Ball Era in which the league got on base at a worse clip were 2013-2015, 1988, 1971-1972, and 1963-1968. This is all happening despite the aforementioned evolution of the science of hitting. It's happening despite a shift in approach and focus, one that would steer OBP ever higher, if only it were working.

Instead, it's sitting at a low ebb, and while it does so, even guys who get on base often are a little less helpful than they were 10 years ago—or 20, or 40, or 60, or 70, or 80, or 90. They're less helpful, that is, because unless there happen to be three or four other guys in the lineup who get on just as regularly, their contribution is merely to forestall the inevitable. Runs happen, increasingly, when a sudden bang happens, and that means attacking early in the count—because pitchers are sure as hell doing that.

In a league making contact on barely 75 percent of its swings, and a league in which an increasing number of pitchers can throw multiple off-speed pitches for strikes in any count, the only way to consistently generate offense is going to be aggressive. This isn't necessarily true for individuals, like Mookie Betts and Jose Ramirez, who make a lot of contact and have excellent plate discipline, and whose power comes from such natural quickness in a short stroke. Most players have to make tradeoffs, though, whether it be lowering their contact rate or raising their chase rate, in order to consistently make the quality of contact necessary to survive in today's game.

Highest %	Lowest %
Javier Baez – 48.3	Joe Mauer – 4.6
Freddie Freeman – 47.1	Mookie Betts – 9.7
Ozzie Albies – 46.3	Brett Gardner – 10.7
Jose Altuve – 44.2	Jose Ramirez – 12.0
Nick Castellanos – 44.1	Jason Kipnis – 13.8
Joey Gallo – 42.3	Jesus Aguilar – 14.5
Corey Dickerson – 40.9	Xander Bogaerts – 15.8
Salvador Perez – 40.8	Brian Dozier – 16.3
Eddie Rosario – 40.7	Mike Trout – 17.6
Nick Ahmed – 40.4	Yasmani Grandal – 17.6

Top 10 and Bottom 10 Hitters, First-Pitch Swing Rate (2018)

The question isn't which of these lists one prefers, but what they each convey, qualitatively, about the cat-and-mouse game of early-count hitting. Those top five on the left, especially, drive home the fact that for most players, getting aggressive early in the count is now key to keeping strikeout rate down and hitting for power.

For now, the message is: pitchers are coming right after batters with the nastiest stuff they've ever had. Batters had better stop giving away strike one and force hurlers to adjust, or the global OBP crisis is only going to get worse.

—*Matthew Trueblood is an author of Baseball Prospectus.*

A Hymn for the Index Stat

Patrick Dubuque

We survived without computers. I know this, because I remember the day when my dad hooked up his brand-new Atari 400 computer to the back of our 12-inch Magnavox television, and the perfect blue of the memo pad lit up for the first time. I was born just on the edge of that transitional generation, of learning cursive and balancing checkbooks and just doing math all the time, constant manual arithmetic.

It still amazes me. We learned how to sail ships without computers. We learned how to do calculus. We built towers that didn't fall down, most of the time. We engineered catapults to knock them down anyway. We built a robust system of philosophy called "utilitarianism," founded on the principle that the good of an action is evaluated by summing the effects of that action, which is the kind of formula that would make the world's mainframes crash. The whole foundation of statistics as a field is "here's math you could easily do but would die of old age first."

The fact of the matter is that there is too much math in the world to do. There are too many things changing, and too many things too small to notice, for us to handle. At some point, they become too much for the computers to handle as well, which is why we have chaos theory and undetectable earthquakes, but it's not an even fight. At some point, we fall back on intuition, and given how under-equipped we are, we're forced to bestow that intuition with some sort of supernatural superiority, the "gut feeling," that we can't prove because we can only intuit that our intuition is better.

We're all lousy at intuition, and wonderful at lying to ourselves about it. The honest truth is that computers are far better at intuition than we are, because in order to know what feels "off" you have to know what's "on." In order to do that you have to constantly reassess the average of everything, then re-rank your own experience against it.

Test your own, by comparing these three anonymous lines:

Player	G	HR	AVG	OBP	SLG
Player A	156	38	.259	.342	.535
Player B	154	38	.280	.348	.527
Player C	158	38	.266	.343	.509

These all seem like pretty similar players, right? The second one a touch more batted-ball dependent, the third a little less strong, but all pretty good hitters. And you'd be right, about the latter. Not the former.

Here's the breakdown:

- Player A: 1991 Howard Johnson, 141 DRC+
- Player B: 1996 Dean Palmer, 121 DRC+
- Player C: 2018 Giancarlo Stanton, 114 DRC+

Baseball is fortunate to have escaped the seismic shifts of so many other sports, where the talents and performances of other eras are nearly unrecognizable. (And not just other sports: try to explain the greatness of the movie Duck Soup without adjusting for era.) But they're still there, and they're nearly impossible to account for manually, without having to resort to sweeping generalizations like "steroid era" or juiced-ball era" to throw out entire swathes of production.

This is all to say that we should celebrate the index stat, that simple 100-based scale with such a humble aim: just to give context. It's hard to imagine how we lived without them for so long. Sabermetricians have always tried to make their stats look like other stats: True Average mapped to batting average, FIP molded to look like and compare to ERA. It's easy to understand the motivation—these statistics carry an emotional value in them that is hard to resist, as with the .300 hitter and the 2.00 ERA—but even they fall prey to the same loss of scale as their unadjusted counterparts. If a .300 average means different things in different years, does that hold true for a .300 True Average?

Instead, 100 doesn't say anything, except above average or below. And it does it instantly, for every season in every run environment for any statistic we want it to. We should have more index stats: K%+, so we can stop comparing Mike Clevinger's career 9.46 K/9 to Nolan Ryan's 9.55. HBP%+, so we can note that Ron Hunt was getting plunked when nobody else was getting plunked, as opposed to that imitator Brandon Guyer. Some might note how stale these references are and accuse league-adjustment as a backward-looking drive, and this is true. But we're always looking backward, always comparing the new with the expectations already set. The index stat just forces us to be honest.

There's always resistance to a new statistic, especially one so outwardly simple and so internally complex. We tend to stick with what we know, even in the case of formulas that are supposed to tell us what we know. But if your resistance is that it seems too complicated, too counterintuitive, too "black boxy," I encourage you to consider why you feel that way. Because the real world is infinitely more complicated than baseball, where all the pitches go in one basic direction and the baserunners are only allowed to travel in four directions. Baseball statistics based on mixed methodology are almost impossibly intricate. So are skyscrapers and automobiles. That's why we have computers—to take the guesswork out of them.

—*Patrick Dubuque is an author of Baseball Prospectus.*

Index of Names

Alexander, Scott	40	May, Dustin	79, 87
Alvarez, Yadier	78, 96	McCreery, Adam	84
Baez, Pedro	42	Muncy, Max	28
Barnes, Austin	18	Orlando, Paulo	83
Bellinger, Cody	20	Pederson, Joc	30
Buehler, Walker	44	Peters, DJ	73, 92
Chargois, J.T.	84	Pollock, A.J.	32
Cingrani, Tony	46	Quackenbush, Kevin	84
Downs, Jeter	83, 94	Rincon, Carlos	74
Estevez, Omar	70	Rios, Edwin	83, 94
Ferguson, Caleb	48	Ruiz, Keibert	75, 88
Floro, Dylan	50	Ryu, Hyun-jin	64
Freese, David	22	Santana, Dennis	80, 90
Gale, Rocky	83	Sborz, Josh	84
Garcia, Yimi	84	Schultz, Jaime	66
Gonsolin, Tony	84, 91	Seager, Corey	34
Gray, Josiah	93	Sheffield, Jordan	84, 96
Hart, Donnie	52	Smith, Will	76, 89
Heredia, Starling	83	Smoker, Josh	84
Hernandez, Enrique	24	Stewart, Brock	84
Hill, Rich	54	Stripling, Ross	68
Jansen, Kenley	56	Taylor, Chris	36
Kasowski, Marshall	84	Toles, Andrew	83
Kelly, Joe	58	Turner, Justin	38
Kendall, Jeren	71, 94	Urias, Julio	81
Kershaw, Clayton	60	Verdugo, Alex	77, 87
Lux, Gavin	72, 90	White, Mitch	82, 92
Maeda, Kenta	62	Wong, Connor	83, 95
Martin, Russell	26		

Ballpark diagrams for Baseball Prospectus are created by THIRTY81Project, a design concept offering original ballpark artwork, including the new 'Ballparks of 2019' 11 x 17 color print.

Visit **www.thirty81project.com** for full details.

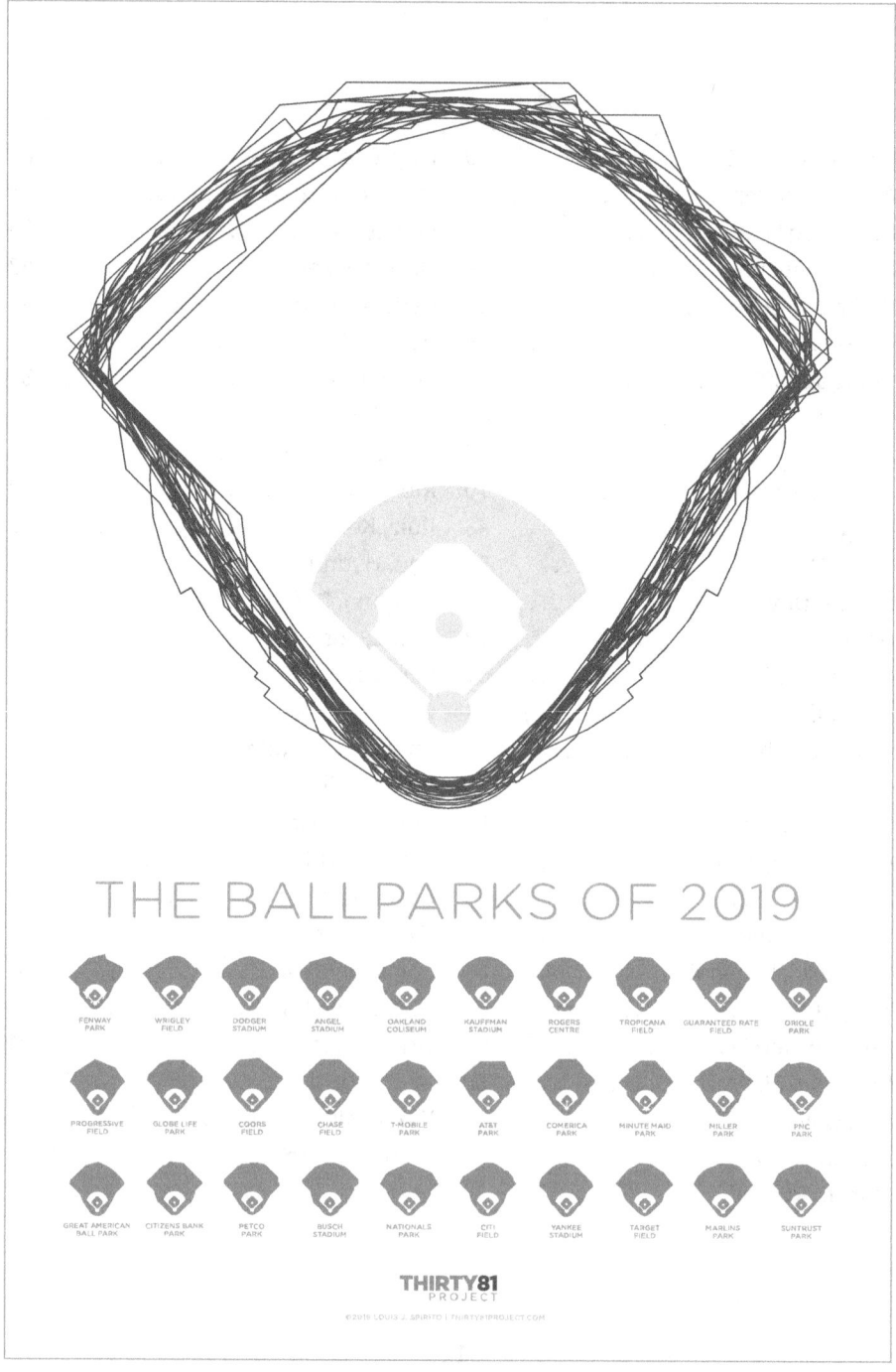